Mindy McIntosh

Cultivate Wealth

Reap the Financial Harvest of Your Hard Work With Your FOCUS Wealth Plan

Copyright © 2024 by Mindy McIntosh.

All rights reserved. No part of this publication may be reproduced, distributed or transmitted in any form or by any means, including photocopying, recording, or other electronic or mechanical methods, without the prior written permission of the publisher, except in the case of brief quotations embodied in critical reviews and certain other noncommercial uses permitted by copyright law.

For permission requests, write to the publisher, addressed "Attention: Permissions Coordinator," at the address below.

Mindy McIntosh/McIntosh & Associates
8282 Midland Road
Freeland, MI 48623
www.wealthmichigan.com

Book Layout ©2013 BookDesignTemplates.com

Ordering Information:
Quantity sales. Special discounts are available on quantity purchases by corporations, associations, and others. For details, contact the "Special Sales Department" at the address above.

Cultivate Wealth/Mindy McIntosh. — 2nd edition
ISBN 9798304863681

Contents

Foreword i

It's Not Where You Start That Matters 1

The FOCUS Process 9

Analysis: What's on the Road Ahead? 15

Strategies: Health Care Planning 21

Strategies: Planning for Lifelong Income 35

Strategies: Reduce the Bite of Taxes 53

Strategies: Why Take the Risk? 73

Strategies: Fill in the Family Circle 87

Implementation: Put Your Plan into Motion 99

Updates: When Occasional Change is Necessary 105

Picking Your Team, and Why It Should Be Us 111

Acknowledgments 119

McIntosh & Associates Financial, LLC is an independent financial services firm that utilizes a variety of investment and insurance products. Mindy McIntosh is a licensed insurance professional. Nolan McIntosh offers investment services. Investment advisory services made available through AE Wealth Management, LLC (AEWM). AEWM and McIntosh and Associates Financial, LLC are not affiliated companies. Investment advisory products and services made available through AE Wealth Management, LLC (AEWM), a Registered Investment Advisor. Insurance products are offered through the insurance business McIntosh and Associates. AEWM does not offer insurance products. The insurance products offered by McIntosh and Associates are not subject to Investment Advisor requirements. AEWM and McIntosh and Associates are not affiliated companies.

Investing involves risk, including the potential loss of principal. No investment strategy can guarantee a profit or protect against loss in periods of declining values. None of the information contained in this book shall constitute an offer to sell or solicit any offer to buy a security or any insurance product.

Neither the firm nor its agents or representatives may give tax or legal advice. Individuals should consult with a qualified professional for guidance before making any purchasing decisions.

Any references to protection benefits or steady and reliable income streams refer only to fixed insurance products. They do not refer, in any way, to securities or investment advisory products. Annuity guarantees are backed by the financial strength and claims-paying ability of the issuing insurance company. Annuities are insurance products that may be subject to fees, surrender charges and holding periods which vary by insurance company. Annuities are not FDIC insured.

The information presented here is not intended to be used as the sole basis for financial decisions, nor should it be construed as advice designed to meet the particular needs of an individual's situation.

We do not offer every plan available in your area. Any information we provide is limited to those plans we do offer in your area. Please contact Medicare.gov or 1-800-MEDICARE to get information on all of your options.

McIntosh & Associates Financial, LLC is not affiliated with the U.S. government, federal Medicare program or any other governmental agency.

Please remember that converting an employer plan account to a Roth IRA is a taxable event. Increased taxable income from the Roth IRA conversion may have several consequences. Be sure to consult with a qualified tax advisor before mak-ing any decisions regarding your IRA.

2651353 11/24

Foreword

By Lorie Krohn

I don't think I'm the only person who often finds it more interesting to explore "why" people do the things they do in life than "how" they go about doing them.

Take, for example, the motivation of Mindy McIntosh, the author of this book. "Why" she does what she does at McIntosh and Associates, her central Michigan financial services firm, is a more interesting story—to me, anyway—than "how" she works to help improve the lives of clients she regards as family.

Of course, Mindy's motivation in life should be of greater interest to me. I am, after all, her mom.

This isn't an easy thing for a mom to say, but Mindy—along with her father, brother, and me—didn't have an easy life growing up on our Michigan farm. Needless to say, farming is a tough life on the best of days, and we didn't have a lot of those. Weather, fluctuating crop prices, and rising costs for feed, fuel, and fertilizer make farming an uncertain lifestyle in which bills often pile up higher than a grain silo.

From the time Mindy was a very young girl—when she was eight, nine, ten—she took responsibilities usually given to a much older child. She was cooking meals, cleaning the house, and doing farm chores. Her Dad worked very hard, as did her brother. I was working two jobs at the time, so Mindy basically ran the household, something she handled with great grace.

When she was just twelve, she got her first real job at an ostrich farm some two miles from home. She began by gathering and incubating ostrich eggs, but within a year she was essentially running the farm. She learned to handle responsibility very early on, and she handled it very well.

But she also watched her father and I go through a lot of financial hardships that she describes in her introductory chapter. We would eventually lose the farm and the equipment that had been in my husband's family for years.

This was very disheartening to Mindy. She wondered if we would be able to stay in our home, something we worked so hard to do. She wondered if she could go to college, her long-time goal.

But Mindy didn't let a slow start in life hold her down. She worked hard to get herself through college, then began working in the field of health care insurance. In time, she started her own company, and later encouraged her husband Nolan to join her.

Today, McIntosh and Associates' mission is to help others improve their current financial situation—whether prosperous or bleak—and realize the best life possible for themselves. Helping people out of the kind of situation she knew as a young girl—or avoiding it entirely—has become Mindy's "why" in helping others as much as she helped me.

Yes, I am more than Mindy's mom. I also happen to be her client.

There once was a time, back on the farm, when I thought I would have to work for the rest of my life just to maintain any kind of standard of living. It was a scary thought.

I was working in a hospital at the time, and we didn't get much guidance in making investment allocations in our retirement plan. That's when I asked Mindy for help. She and Nolan assisted me in making some better choices. We also talked about the kind of lifestyle I envisioned, and what I might do to help me get there.

I went from having a future that didn't look so bright, one in which I thought I might have to work until well into my seventies or older, to one where I now look forward to retiring very soon in my early sixties. I'm looking forward to spending more time with my grandkids—her three kids—in the very near future. That's my "why" for doing the things I do today.

I guess what I'm trying to say in all this is that where you are now shouldn't dictate where you will be in the future. You may be down right now, or think you are, but with the proper guidance from the right people, you can improve your situation by getting the help you need with whatever it takes—life insurance, health care insurance, saving and investing advice.

I've seen people come into our office—and yes, I now work with Mindy and Nolan and our team—very nervous about their ability to retire at the time they would like to do so. And I've seen many leave feeling better about their situation after learning of things they could do to help make their retirement dream a reality, or changes that need to be made to make it happen.

We often encounter people who come from backgrounds of starting with very little, or others who've lost almost everything. Mindy understands their situation. She knows the pain and uncertainty they might be experiencing because she's been in the ditch herself and worked her way out of it. She believes there is light at the end of every tunnel and that opportunities exist for everyone.

This, I believe, is her "why" for all she does today to help people improve their financial lives. This, I believe, is why she wrote this book.

INTRODUCTION

It's Not Where You Start That Matters

Most people would like to think that retirement life is easy, that "the golden years" after working for decades and maybe raising a family should be the time when we do the things we've long put off doing because of other obligations or dedication.

I won't argue with that. Retirement should be about making time for yourself and realizing some of your long-standing dreams now that you have the chance to live them.

After all, there's no more demand to show up to work at a certain time. Your kids, if you had any, are most likely grown with careers and families of their own. Maybe you've paid off your mortgage and have less debt than when you were paying off student loans—your own or your kids' college loans—or paying for the two cars you needed when you were a two-income family. Maybe you'll downsize and putter more around your yard or garage. Maybe you'll spend more time with your grandkids. Maybe you'll travel more, see places you once only talked about visiting. Now that you're not running a business or on someone else's time clock, maybe you'll volunteer at a local charitable organization, catch up on your reading, or take up a new recreational activity or hobby. Maybe you'll do all of that and more.

But here's a reality check: That idyllic retirement life doesn't just happen. It takes planning in the years leading up to when you can finally claim time as your own. Planning and financing your golden years is a complicated undertaking that we believe you shouldn't do alone. And you don't need to.

I often hear people say, "I wish someone would have told me." And I get it. It's the reason I wrote this book. You see, I want to be the person who tells you things you'll eventually be glad you learned earlier.

Allow me to introduce myself. I'm Mindy McIntosh, founder and president of McIntosh and Associates, my financial services company in the central Michigan community of Freeland. I've spent my professional career and built my business addressing the many things people "wish someone had told me earlier." This is especially the case when dealing with retirement issues that far too many people are unprepared to handle.

Look, I understand why we often put off planning for a time that seems a long way down our life's road. We get so consumed by the here and now that looking too far into the future gets pushed to the side. Months, years, and eventually decades go by, and before we know it, retirement is looming just ahead on the horizon.

Suddenly, something close to panic seeps in.

Where did the time go? Is it too late to plan for my retirement? Is it too late to still dream? Do I have enough money to retire now, or will I be working years longer than I'd hoped? Do I have the kind of retirement savings that will last as long as I do? What do I need to know about Social Security and Medicare, and what in the world is a Required Minimum Distribution? How will I pick a plan and pay for health care? And what will happen to me if I need nursing home assistance? Can I afford it, or will I become a burden on my family?

These are all good questions. I plan to address all of them in the following pages.

Again, I get why there is such a lack of knowledge about what it takes to plan for retirement and live the life you deserve. I hear it from people all the time. Maybe you don't know where to go to find the information or guidance you need. Maybe you question whether there's someone in the financial service industry who can really understand your unique situation, and who appreciates that the financial struggle you experience as you juggle your family and career is real. Well, I do. Allow me to explain why.

My cash-crop background

My brother and I grew up on a cash-crop farm in Michigan where Dad managed and worked endlessly on the farm while Mom worked as a licensed practical nurse. They knew hard work. They knew sacrifice. They lived day-to-day without a lot of thought about years down the road, much less to a time when they would not be working.

My brother and I were expected to help out—running equipment, cooking and feeding the crew, doing chores, and pitching in wherever we could. We were a family of modest means, and we were careful about our spending. We didn't have a lot of extras, but we always approached everything as a team, tackling what needed to be done. And yes, sometimes the bills and debts piled up.

Looking back, I see now that my parents were under a lot of stress. I have built upon their experiences as a motivation for what I do today. If I can help someone avoid some of the problems and insecurity they faced, I will have had a good day.

With our financial condition varying from crop to crop—some good years, some not so great—my parents didn't have anything close to what you would call a retirement plan. My father was like many farmers, God bless them all. He had no exit plan, other than to work until he could work no more. It was hard, manual labor. But his work ethic defined who he was, and I know many people in rural America just like him. My mom put away whatever she could into a retirement plan, but she always knew it wasn't enough.

My family's generations of farming came to a halt when my dad had to sell his portion of the farm. Times got tough, and it was hard to make it. My parents downsized from the farmhouse and forty acres of land to about a two-acre lot with a home, and Dad went to work for a trucking company while still maintaining his love of farming on the side.

It's been said that when life throws you a curveball, you need a Plan B. For my parents, that breaking ball came when Dad started his fight against cancer. This showed up just about the time he finally was almost out of debt. Our family home was paid for, and he was starting to slow down to become more work-optional focused. I consider myself truly blessed that I had enough experience in the insurance industry by then to get them into a health insurance plan, and later Medicare for Dad. I'm sad to report that we lost him in 2021.

On a brighter note, my mom is planning to retire in the next year or so, and she has confidence that she will be able to live out the lifestyle of her choice in retirement. This choice just might mean spending countless fun hours with our three daughters. She truly adores the kids and they bring pure joy and purpose to Mom's life.

I point all this out not to pat myself or my parents on the back for preparing for the kind of financial distress that can befall any of us at any time. Instead, I would note how I learned from my own experience that it's never too late to develop a plan to support yourself during tough times of economic or medical hardship. Such a plan can go a long way to help alleviate the feelings of helplessness that can arise in such times. I am truly blessed to have been raised in such a loving and supportive family, to be part of a team that always said if I had a desire to do something, then go for it, but be all in.

Helping the people of my roots

In 1998, I went off to college at Michigan State University. I thought I was going to be a veterinarian or maybe work in the pharmaceutical industry serving vets. But I switched up after thinking about how the life of a vet often deals with sadness. (I just don't believe I have it in me to put down Old Yeller.) So, at age twenty-two, I started working in the finance and insurance field.

As I started working with clients, I found I could relate to the lives of so many of them. The stories they told and the concerns they expressed were the same as many I had experienced, even at a young age.

These were middle-class Americans just like my parents. Many were people who, despite their college degrees, hard work, and modest spending habits, sometimes struggled to make ends meet. They had kids they wanted to send to college. They were paying off their homes. They were planning family vacations. Retirement seemed like a far-off thing. They had an idea of what they wanted to do in retirement, but as we dug into their financial lives, they came to realize that retirement life wasn't going to materialize unless they put together a plan—a process for saving, investing, and accomplishing goals—and started making some hard decisions.

Statistics, however, show us that too many of these hard-working people aren't planning. Too many are still trying to figure out how to finance their lives today, much less their retirement lives in the future. One survey indicated that nearly 70 percent of Americans have saved less than $100,000 for their retirement.[1]

Why is this? In my opinion, it's largely a lack of knowledge. Many financial professionals say too many Americans don't understand how to save, when to do it, and how much savings they might need for retirement. Some seem to think we are still in a time when retirees could count on a reliable pension combined with Social Security and personal savings to provide all the retirement income they need. Today, however, that picture looks very different. Pensions are increasingly rare, and the future of Social Security is unclear, leaving many people to rely more on their savings and personal investments.

I knew from personal experience what can happen to those who don't plan. My parents, after all, were among those who said to me, "I wish someone had told me." I'd also watched an aunt struggle to care for

---

[1] Ashleigh Ray. Go Banking Rates. June 22, 2022. "Have Less Than $100K Saved for Retirement? Here's How To Catch Up" https://www.aol.com/less-100k-saved-retirement-catch-110014532.html

her father-in-law after he developed dementia and had no means to pay for the skilled nursing care he required.

Those experiences, and the desire to help others avoid them, are among the reasons I founded my company, now known as McIntosh and Associates.

It's all about family

I love the outdoors and doing fun, physical activities with my family. My husband, Nolan, had a career in physical therapy and athletic training before he joined me in the company. He had a successful career, having earned a doctorate of physical therapy. But he later switched his career field. Part of his reason for doing so was that we could spend more time together and with our kids, helping to coach their sports teams and not miss a thing. But he also shares a belief we both hold dear. That is, financial wellness is just as important as physical wellness.

You might be thinking there's a theme here, and there is. The concept of "family" has always been very important to me and has significantly influenced my career. This is why our company continues to focus on the everyday middle-class families and individuals who have dreams of being able to retire and enjoy life.

We work to bring confidence, comfort, and clarity to these people. We try to do that by developing plans and strategies that create retirement income designed to last as long as they do. We work to help ensure they have an approach in place to help provide necessary funding for medical care when needed, and we help them choose the health care policies that are right for them. We work to help provide funding for long-term care should it become necessary, as it will be for many Americans. We work to develop a strategy to help deal with new taxes that become quickly apparent in retirement. We work to develop ways to help provide ongoing support for a surviving spouse or other loved ones when we are no longer here.

Our process for creating customized retirement and investment plans that are unique to each family is called the FOCUS Wealth Plan.

It features five basic components: FOCUS, analysis, strategies, implementation, and updates. These are all part of a comprehensive process, one that involves far more than just setting aside money. We'll look at each part in separate chapters throughout this book.

Our "strategies" discussion will include five distinct areas: health care planning, income planning, risk tolerance and wealth management, tax-saving strategies, and legacy planning.

In writing this book and using other media (group presentations, radio/TV interviews, and more), I hope to curb this lack of knowledge about retirement and investment planning. Of course, the book you hold is not an exhaustive list of every available financial solution, but my goal is to discuss some of the most common ways we can help people address their challenges with money. Too many people simply don't know what they don't know. Let's change that.

Planning for retirement can be complicated, but if you work with a knowledgeable retirement professional, it doesn't have to be daunting or overwhelming.

Sure, sometimes this involves addressing major concerns about future income or resolving current debt. But other times, a goal is just to help people find the financial peace of mind to know that they don't have to go to work every day when it's physically hard for them to do so, or to work two jobs just to make ends meet. Other people simply want to free up more time for themselves. Time to be active with the grandkids while they are still healthy enough to enjoy them. Time to help an elderly parent who needs assistance. Time to travel, if that's a goal, or to relocate and seek a different lifestyle.

The key in doing all of this, however, involves having a plan. At McIntosh and Associates, we believe that by giving people information they can understand and the financial tools they need, we can work together to build such a plan—one unique to their individual situation—that can help them do many of the things they want to in retirement when more of your time is your own.

This is the difference, we believe, between just envisioning what retirement *should be* and realizing what it truly *can be*.

CHAPTER 1

The FOCUS Process

You may recall from the introduction chapter that my husband and business partner, Nolan, previously worked in physical therapy before we joined forces in McIntosh and Associates. I generally leave most discussions of physical ailments or injuries to him, the expert in the family.

Even so, Nolan won't correct me if I say there is no way in the world that an orthopedic surgeon would perform a major surgery—say, replacing a hip or a torn anterior cruciate ligament—without first ordering an MRI exam or some other deep-dive radiology look at the body part needing repair.

Along those same lines, I can't say I could immediately trust a mechanic who starts talking about lifting the entire engine block without first running diagnostic checks to see why engine oil is leaking.

Now, I'm not suggesting that an experienced mechanic doesn't have good gut-instinct ideas about what is needed for a car repair. Still, when it comes to helping people manage their money, we prefer to operate like a skilled surgeon.

My license allows me to provide insurance strategies for the people we work with, and as an Investment Adviser Representative, Nolan offers planning and advisory services. We each have specific knowledge that allows us to meet each client's specific needs. Some may leave with a full plan that covers investments and others may simply need insurance products that cover them in case of an emergency later in life.

Same goes for someone suffering a serious medical condition such as cancer. You would need to seek out a medical specialist in your particular type of cancer and treatment rather than relying exclusively on a primary care general practitioner.

Understanding the concerns or problems we will be trying to address is why the FOCUS process is the essential first step in building our FOCUS Wealth Plan. This comprehensive system, unique to each client(s), is designed to provide retirement confidence and preservation through the development and implementation of lifelong income plans, health care, and nursing care options, managing risk while continuing to grow wealth in retirement, dealing with taxes and planning for the ongoing support of loved ones when we are no longer here to do so. More on all of that is coming later in this book.

The first step in doing any of these things, however, is first learning about you and where you want to go before deciding on the best way to get there.

Where are we headed?

The first meeting with any new client(s) involves more listening than talking on our part. We'll explain what you need to know about us, to be sure, but we're more interested in learning about you.

Among the many things we want to know:

What are your financial concerns, either with your situation now or in the future? What are your goals, your dreams for retirement? What are your essential needs? Are you ambitious with hopes of living well, or are you content to live well within your means?

More specifically, tell us about the scope of your retirement dreams. Are you wanting to visit all the capitals of Europe, or are your travel plans more domestic in nature? (I'm told that Austin is also an interesting capital city. And Nashville, and Santa Fe.) Do you dream of visiting the pyramids of the Upper Nile, or might you be just as happy spending your newfound time closer to home at, say, a vacation home in the Upper Peninsula? These kinds of different aspirations typically weigh heavily on the level of retirement income we will work to provide.

But there are many other areas to explore.

Here in central Michigan, for instance, the idea of being a "snowbird" is popular among people anxious to escape our often-harsh winters. Might this be you? Do you dream of a second home in Florida perhaps, or a regular extended stay in Arizona? Perhaps you're considering a more permanent relocation to another part of the country where the lifestyle (and climate) is different? This, too, will require adjustments in your long-term income planning.

What is your current health situation? What kind of concerns do you have about your future health based on your family history? These are certainly factors that must be considered when thinking about what kind of resources you will require in retirement.

What kind of risk are you willing to take in the future growth of your retirement assets? A little? A lot? None at all? This is information we will need before designing a retirement investment strategy for the continued growth of money you will most likely need later in life.

What are your biggest concerns about retirement? Is it running out of money? Is it being able to live independently and without having to rely on family assistance? Is it being able to leave a legacy gift for loved ones? Is it all of the above? (Yeah, that's what I guessed.)

Our FOCUS process, you must understand, works two ways. We are interviewing you, but you are also interviewing us. You need to determine whether you are comfortable having us offer far-ranging advice on your future. Conversely, we have to decide if we think you are willing to listen to what we have to say. We're going to be going through this together, and if we're going to have a long working relationship—which we hope to have—we need to know if we're a good fit.

Let's be transparent about something else here at the beginning.

If you're looking for a financial advisor who can grow your portfolio by 30 percent over a short period of time, we may not be the people you're looking for. Sure, we provide wealth management and investment advice, as well as insurance options, to people of all ages. But our main focus is on retirement planning. If we can get you started on this process at a younger age, great, let's talk. But if you're looking for guidance on cryptocurrency investment strategies, we probably aren't a good fit.

When the chemistry is right, however—and I'm proud to say it is more often than it isn't—we set up a second meeting where the FOCUS process takes a deeper dive.

What is our starting point?

Once we get an idea of where you want to go, we need to know more about where we are at the starting point.

After a first introductory meeting, after we decide that there will be subsequent discussions, we send people forward with a homework request. (OK, it's more of a homework assignment, but I try to avoid reviving bad school-day memories.) We ask people to bring to a second meeting—if they didn't already do so at the first—copies of investment account statements, bank statements, and recent tax returns.

No, we're not the IRS.

We ask for this material only because we need an idea of where you stand in personal savings and investments— specifically, to know how these assets are positioned for both income and tax purposes. We need a few years of recent tax returns only to learn something about your current tax bracket. This will be important later as we look for opportunities to build up tax-free income sources such as converting current tax-deferred assets into future tax-free ones.

We'll ask to look at any current life insurance coverage. We do this as a starting point before considering whether existing coverage might be improved to provide future tax-free income to you as well as non-taxable death benefits to heirs.

We're especially interested in examining your health insurance, something we consider a priority at our company.

Many pre-retirees we see for the first time likely are still covered by company-offered group health care plans during their working years. That's wonderful, but people know this coverage won't last forever. People retiring "early" will need to explore health insurance options before Medicare kicks in at age sixty-five. People on Medicare also have decisions to make about supplemental policies that cover what Medicare doesn't. We stand ready and eager to help in this process. In doing so, it helps to know what kind of coverage you need and are accustomed to, the premiums you pay, the co-pays and deductibles you can manage.

We'll talk about these aspects in much greater detail in the upcoming chapter on health care coverage.

What do you actually spend?
What do you actually earn?

We'll also begin an in-depth look at your current and projected future household budget, an essential first step in your retirement income planning process.

This budget "homework assignment" is one of the most detailed parts of the FOCUS process. For while most people can "guesstimate" what they spend each month—our mortgage or rent is known; our utility bill averages this; our home and car insurance is that; we spend this on groceries and that on dining/entertainment; our monthly credit card bill averages X and we still have a car payment of Y—they rarely go into the kind of detail needed to determine the essential living expenses they should expect in retirement. This is important information to know as you prepare for a time of life when you must provide your own paychecks to pay for your routine costs of everyday living.

That's why our "Confidential Financial Profile" features a monthly budget worksheet that goes much deeper than most people do. It looks at (among many other things) your monthly cell phone bill, internet costs, personal property taxes, water/sewage charges, shopping expenses, recreational activities, club and HOA memberships, home upkeep, prescription medications, child care expenses, vet bills...

Yeah, it can seem exhausting. But it's an invaluable fact-finding mission that, frankly, more families might consider doing if only to get a more accurate picture of what they actually spend each month.

Your confidential personal profile also looks at income—what you have coming in now while still working, and what you might expect in retirement when the employment paychecks stop and you begin the process of paying yourself. Among multiple income prospects to consider:

How much can you expect to receive from Social Security? (The Social Security Administration offers a helpful calculator at www.ssa.gov.) Will you have pension income or rental income? Might annuity income figure into the equation? What is your current balance in retirement investment plans such as a 401(k), 403(b), traditional IRA, or tax-advantageous Roth IRA? What do you have in available cash should an emergency arise?

We'll talk later about how much might be taken each year from personal investments and savings in order to meet living expenses not filled by Social Security or other "fixed income" sources.

Again, the FOCUS process can be very detailed. But when it's done, you will have gained as much valuable insight into yourself as we have of you. This is information you will need whether you do your future retirement planning with us (as we hope), with someone else, or (and I hesitate to say this) on your own.

With McIntosh and Associates, however, the process is just beginning. Next, we'll examine what we do with all this information as we look ahead at both the potential peaks and valleys of your impending retirement.

CHAPTER 2

Analysis: What's on the Road Ahead?

We've now likely spent two full meetings learning about you and your hopes, your dreams, and your current financial status. We appreciate your honesty and thoroughness during this process. We appreciate the trust you've placed in us. You've told us where you want to go, and we can see the big picture.

Now let us be your tour guide on the road to retirement. Allow us to describe what we see ahead on your journey, the scenic viewpoints as well as any potential pitfalls.

This is the Analysis part of building your FOCUS Wealth Plan. This is our chance to show you where we believe you are today, where we think you can go tomorrow—as well as ten, twenty, thirty, or more years from now—and how we can make the road ahead as smooth as possible,

This is where we take all the information you've provided and put it into perspective. This is where we first begin to answer some key questions. Among them:

Given the opportunity to walk away from your job tomorrow, would you? Could you? Are you in a position to retire this year, next year, or five years from now? Or must your retirement dreams be put off until some later point? What parts of your current financial structure are going to need tweaking before, or right after, retirement arrives? What things need to be added to meet future income needs? Are you adequately insured, especially for health care? Do you need to take more risk in the growth of your assets? Do you need to take less?

I know, it seems like I'm still asking questions. In reality, however, these are questions we are now prepared to answer after a thorough, fact-driven analysis of what you've told us about yourself.

Looking at the big picture

I'm pleased to report that for many of our new clients/friends at McIntosh and Associates, this Analysis portion of our process provides a brighter picture than they initially thought possible.

Many people we see are pleasantly surprised to learn that they've done a better job of preparing for life after the workaday world than they thought. They've saved and invested in their own future—even when it was darned difficult to do so while raising a family and managing a career or business—and now have a nest egg of potential retirement income. (I will pause my typing here as I applaud them.)

They've followed a game plan, and the goal line is within sight. But now their plan may need some fine-tuning. They may, for instance, need guidance on how to take income from their savings. They'll need to look at the best time to begin taking Social Security benefits. They'll want to consider strategies for easing the sting of taxes, for developing a medical insurance plan, and doing some estate planning. But the bottom line is, they could retire now if they choose, and the smiles we see after conveying that news is a big part of why I love my job.

Of course, not all stories have this happy ending.

For people who haven't saved what they could when they could afford to do so, the picture isn't as clear. Life is challenging enough, and putting money away for the future when you need every buck in the here and now isn't always possible. I get that; I lived it. I don't mean to be overly critical of people whose retirement dreams fall short of their reality.

But this is where our Analysis process can provide a wake-up call, perhaps the first many people will receive.

As mentioned earlier, I don't believe it's ever too late to start anything. But that also means starting with a plan, and that plan begins with honest FOCUS and analysis. For it's often only after people see that Social Security alone won't provide the retirement income they need that they consider "catch-up" measures that might be taken.

Here is where we can offer encouragement, even redemption. Here is where we might talk about working a few years longer than planned, or even considering part-time employment in retirement. We can talk about maximizing contributions to retirement savings programs such as the 401(k), IRA, and Roth IRA. We can talk about enhancing one's lifetime Social Security benefit by waiting until age seventy to begin taking it. We might talk about the lifetime income stream offered by an annuity, or the living benefits of some life insurance policies.

There are many things we can talk about to help people climb out of a hole. But we first need to talk and plan how to do it.

Plan to avoid the potholes

Again, there are adjustments that can be made—and sometimes need to be made—both for people who are prepared to retire soon and those who aren't. Our Analysis process takes the information you've provided and looks ahead to possible areas of concern.

- We'll assess your chance of running out of money in retirement. This is the biggest concern expressed by most people we see. Our preliminary analysis employs software to give you an idea of how long your personal savings could last as a supplement to regular, reliable "fixed income streams" such as Social Security or a pension. We will discuss ways of enhancing fixed income, if necessary. Chapter 4 on income planning will examine how anticipated retirement living expenses might be met by "fixed income" supplemented by your personal savings.

- We'll assess the state of your health insurance coverage, knowing that rising medical costs as our bodies age can be a major drain on any pool of retirement savings. We'll look at coverage options both before and after Medicare begins at age sixty-five. We'll also consider your prospects for future medical or long-term nursing needs based on your family history.
- Remembering that every dollar you save in taxes is one more dollar you have to spend, we'll begin some preliminary conversions about tax-saving strategies. Many people know they must start paying taxes eventually on the tax-deferred money they built up over the years in 401(k) and IRA accounts. Using information you provided on your tax returns, we will assess how fully taxable Required Minimum Distributions might affect your future taxes. We'll also discuss ways of potentially reducing their impact by draining the pool of tax-deferred money and converting it into tax-free assets at times when it may be the most tax-advantageous to do so. A more in-depth look at RMDs and the "hidden taxes" of retirement is upcoming in a later chapter.
- We'll assess where you stand with life insurance. We'll look at the coverage you have now—or might consider adding—that might be converted into policies that not only produce tax-free death benefits to loved ones, but also could be a source of tax-free income while you are still with us.
- Using computer software, we'll examine whether the risk in your current investment portfolio is consistent with what you've described as your *risk tolerance*. This is important information to have both before and early into retirement. For while you may not be as anxious to grow your wealth as you were as a younger investor, there is still a need to continue growing your money for future expenses in retirement—most likely health care or nursing care expenses.

The key is to do this at a risk level with which you are comfortable, which we also will explore.
- Might you want to consider lifestyle changes? Is downsizing an option? What about moving to a different part of the country? We might assess the option of turning equity in your home into an income source.
- We'll assess your current debt situation, if any, and explore options for reducing something you don't want to take into retirement.
- If applicable, we can examine effective ways of selling an interest in a business, or continuing in the business at whatever level you desire in retirement. We also might discuss your options for either self- or standard employment in retirement, something you might do because you *want* to do so as opposed to because you *have* to.
- Finally, and never a popular subject, let's begin at least talking about taking care of loved ones who survive you. We'll touch on legacy options such as possibly building a tax-free estate through insurance or gifting, as well as the tax advantages of doing both. Not an easy thought process for many people, but something to consider now while you are still able to do so.

Once we work together to define the adjustments necessary to help smooth out your road into retirement, we can then begin the process of looking at specific improvements. This brings us to the Strategies part of the FOCUS Wealth Plan, which we will discuss in greater detail over the next five chapters.

CHAPTER 3

Strategies: Health Care Planning

I mentioned previously that I spent my earliest years in the financial services industry working with health insurance products. But my appreciation of the safety net that health insurance can provide was developed long before then.

I was in my teens when I watched an aunt struggle with the emotional, physical, and financial difficulties of caring for her father-in-law. He had dementia, but little means to fund the care he needed. The lesson hit home even more dramatically later on during my own father's battle with cancer. His fight incurred medical bills in the tens of thousands of dollars. Fortunately for my mom, I was able to help put them on a path that resulted in the selection of a health insurance plan that helped cover much of those costs and kept her out of any debt following Dad's passing.

The rising costs of health care and finding ways to pay for it are major concerns for many people approaching retirement. And they should be. It's my personal belief that the increasing medical bills we incur from the normal process of aging are often the biggest single drain, especially when viewed with long-term care costs, on retirement savings. This is why the first Strategy in our FOCUS Wealth Plan involves finding adequate health care coverage.

What kind of medical costs might a typical couple encounter throughout retirement?

Well, the 2024 Retirement Health Care Cost Estimate prepared for Fidelity Institutional estimates that a couple at age sixty-five will need as much as $315,000 to cover medical expenses incurred during the course of an average retirement.[2] Keep in mind that this estimate *does not* include costs for possible long-term nursing care but deals only with Medicare premiums, co-pays, co-insurance, and deductibles to be met for doctor and hospital visits and all generic, branded, and specialty prescription drugs.

(Note: A discussion of the costs of long-term nursing care, which is not covered by Medicare or traditional health care insurance, will be included in Chapter 7 on The Family Circle.)

That's a big chunk of cash, a potential pothole on the road to a successful retirement. That kind of expenditure can be a game-changer in the long-term success of any retirement plan.

And yet far too many people we see on an initial visit have little or even no idea of how they will pay for these likely expenses over ten, twenty, thirty-plus years of retirement. Sure, they know a little about Medicare, the government program of health care coverage for Americans age sixty-five and older, but not nearly enough about the limits of this coverage. People routinely ask, "Will we run out of money in retirement?" We often learn that they're not as concerned about what they might spend *voluntarily*, but what they might *have to spend* on health care or long-term care. They need help in protecting themselves from these prospective high costs.

I understand the reason for their worries.

People on the verge of retirement, or in the early stages of it, are entering a largely unknown world. For the thirty to forty years of their working careers, they not only drew a regular paycheck, but likely also received health insurance provided by an employer. They most likely paid only a share of that insurance premium, splitting the cost with their employer.

---

[2] Fidelity Wealth Management. June 20, 2024. "Keys to covering health care in retirement" https://www.fidelity.com/learning-center/wealth-management-insights/how-to-prepare-for-health-care-costs-in-retirement

Now with retirement approaching, things are very different. Not only does the regular paycheck disappear, but so does the health insurance. Suddenly, regular checks and insurance coverage become their responsibility, and many people often feel lost when it comes to making decisions about providing for their own income and medical insurance. They find themselves bombarded by phone calls, TV ads, and mailed material that deals with the unfamiliar alphabet soup of health coverage for seniors. It can be downright overwhelming when they're suddenly looking at fifty different plan choices.

I've personally known people who are so confused about providing for their health care in retirement that they're reluctant to move away from an employer-offered plan and keep working beyond what is necessary. This is sad, especially when all they need is the right team of professionals to explain their options. Professionals, I would suggest, such as the members of my team at McIntosh and Associates.

You've got questions; we've got answers

People looking forward to retirement have questions, lots of them.

How do I sign up for Medicare? What will it cost? What does it cover? What doesn't it cover? How do I pay for the uncovered costs? What's this I hear about deadlines and penalties for doing things incorrectly, or doing them late?

How will we be covered if retiring before age sixty-five? What if I continue working beyond sixty-five and still have my employer coverage? How do I deal with prescription drug costs? Is this coverage included in Medicare? And how is Medicare Advantage, which I hear about in what seems like one in every four TV commercials, different from Medicare Supplements?

This is where we step in.

Helping people deal with their myriad questions involving health care coverage is a big part of what we do at my company. We are proud of our background in insurance matters, which we believe to be a major component of planning for retirement. Consequently, we are eager to help guide people to strategies that can be right for their unique situation. Such planning can be a major differentiator in how much you pay for the same coverage. We take pride in our ability to lay out different coverage options for both pre- and post-retirement years. If you have questions, as most new clients do, we work hard to provide answers, and then work to provide options to serve you.

Let's consider a few examples.

For people leaving the daily workforce (either voluntarily or otherwise) prior to age sixty-five, we might talk about COBRA insurance that allows you continued participation in your employer-provided group coverage for anywhere from eighteen to thirty-six months, the latter being applicable only under special circumstances.[3] This is coverage you will pay for, but it's also the coverage with which you are most familiar. As an alternative, we can explore federally subsidized health insurance provided under the Affordable Care Act. A team member in our office is a certified agent who will help navigate and assist with the tax and subsidy options available through the Health Insurance Marketplace. We can discuss cost-share plans and carrier options, then help you enroll and make a smooth transition into the coverage of your choosing, should that be your choice.

We also help people approaching Medicare age learn about enrollment in Parts A and B. For most people already receiving Social Security benefits, Part A enrollment is automatic (though opt-out provisions exist), with coverage beginning on the first day of the month you turn sixty-five.[4] For people not yet on Social Security, we'll outline the "Initial Enrollment Period," a seven-month period that includes three months before, as well as the month of and three months after the month in which you turn sixty-five.

---

[3] U.S. Department of Labor. 2024. "FAQs on COBRA Continuation Health Coverage for Workers" https://www.dol.gov/sites/dolgov/files/ebsa/about-ebsa/our-activities/resource-center/faqs/cobra-continuation-health-coverage-consumer.pdf

[4] Centers for Medicare and Medicaid Services. September 10, 2024. "Original Medicare (Parts A and B) Eligibility and Enrollment" https://www.cms.gov/Medicare/Eligibility-and-Enrollment/OrigMedicarePartABEligEnrol

We'll explain that Part B has a monthly premium ($174.70 in 2024) that is deducted from each monthly Social Security benefit or paid out-of-pocket by enrollees who are not yet receiving Social Security.[5] We'll note that while Part B is technically optional, there is a lifetime late-enrollment penalty—an additional 10 percent on the monthly premium for each twelve-month period in which you were eligible for Part B but declined to enroll—assessed against those who add this coverage later. We'll talk about how a worker (and spouse) who maintains coverage through an employer plan can avoid this penalty by enrolling within a certain timeline, a "special enrollment period," after ending the employer coverage. We'll talk about how the same rules apply to Part D, prescription drug coverage.

We'll talk about options for covering what Medicare doesn't through the purchase of Medicare supplemental insurance—aka, "Medigap" coverage. We'll also discuss how Advantage plans could provide a less costly alternative to "traditional Medicare" and Medigap coverage.

And there, as promised, we've provided some quick "thumbnail" answers to some of the many questions we encounter every day from new and long-time clients. (You didn't even have to leave the comfort of your favorite reading chair.)

But I'm getting way ahead of myself here. Our look at the health insurance needs of people in retirement goes much, much deeper than the few paragraphs above. Let's begin this more in-depth look with a basic breakdown of the various layers of Medicare.

The A, B, C, and Ds of Medicare

Medicare, the principal source of health insurance for American seniors, consists of four parts, A through D. For our discussion here, we'll set aside Part C—Medicare Advantage—until after our brief

---

[5] Centers for Medicare & Medicaid Services. October 11, 2023. "2024 Medicare Parts A & B Premiums and Deductibles"
https://www.rrb.gov/Newsroom/NewsReleases/MedicarePartBPremium#

discussion of the other components of what is often called "traditional Medicare."

Part A: Hospital coverage

Part A is commonly known as "hospital coverage." It covers inpatient hospital charges (though not those of physicians practicing there) when you are an overnight patient whose admission has been ordered by a doctor. (An emergency room visit is not covered by Part A, but is included in Part B coverage.) Part A also covers a limited stay in a skilled nursing facility, but does not cover custodial or long-term nursing care. Part A also covers hospice and some home health care.

Part A has an annual deductible of $1,632 in 2024, after which charges on a hospital stay of up to sixty days are covered. Co-insurance charges of $408 per day (in 2024) are assessed on stays that exceed sixty days.[6]

Most people have already paid the premium for Part A coverage through the Medicare tax included in FICA withholdings from our regular paychecks. In 2024, the Medicare tax of 1.45 percent is paid by both the employee and an employer, and a self-employed person pays as both.[7] People without a history of paying this tax must pay the Part A premium out-of-pocket.[8]

Part B: Outpatient medical coverage

Part B covers (in part) charges from physicians and other providers for outpatient medical care. It also covers (among other things) ambulance calls, preventive and diagnostic services, laboratory charges, mental health services, rehabilitation equipment, and limited home

---

[6] Ibid.
[7] Tina Orem. NerdWallet. May 8, 2024. "FICA Tax: Definition and How It Works in 2024" https://www.nerdwallet.com/article/taxes/fica-tax-withholding
[8] The Part A monthly premium in 2024 was $505 for people who paid Medicare taxes for less than thirty quarters. That premium was reduced to $278 for people who paid Medicare taxes for between thirty and thirty-nine quarters. Source: Centers for Medicare & Medicaid Services. 2024. "Costs" https://www.medicare.gov/basics/costs/medicare-costs

health care. But after meeting an annual deductible ($240 in 2024), Part B generally covers only 80 percent of such charges.[9] For many people, these unpaid charges precipitate the need for supplemental coverage, a subject we will explore later in this chapter.

Part B has a monthly premium of $174.70 in 2024.[10] Note, too, that higher earners face an even-higher monthly Part B premium, technically known as the Income Related Monthly Adjustment Amount (IRMAA). The amount of this surcharge is based on an individual or couple's modified adjusted gross income (MAGI) of two years earlier. In 2024, married couples with a MAGI over $206,000 and individuals with a MAGI over $103,000 will pay an additional amount on their Part B and Part D premiums. For example, a MAGI greater than $161,000 and less than $193,001 would be $279.50 (Part B) and $53.80 (Part D). Those same MAGI amounts apply to married couples with MAGI of about $322,000 and less than $386,001.[11] And there are two other IRMAA step-up levels beyond that.

As noted above, Part B coverage is optional, but I don't advise trying to go without it.

You sometimes hear people talk of handling their routine medical expenses without needing health insurance. Congrats to them (I suppose). But doing this in retirement isn't so easy when our bodies begin to wear down. Someone facing a major heart surgery or knee replacement may suddenly want Medicare coverage, only to find they must pay a 10 percent penalty on every future monthly premium for every year they could have had this coverage but chose not to take it. As I said, I don't recommend trying to "time" this system.

At the same time, though, people having what Medicare calls "creditable coverage," such as that provided by an employer to a worker (and spouse), can avoid Part B enrollment for as long as they are covered by a plan that provides all (or more) than Medicare does. When this

---

[9] Ibid.
[10] Ibid.
[11] Donna LeValley. Kiplinger. August 27, 2024. "Medicare Premiums 2024: IRMAA for Parts B and D" https://www.kiplinger.com/retirement/medicare/medicare-premiums-2024-irmaa-for-parts-b-and-d#:

coverage ends—i.e., when a worker retires or otherwise leaves the job—there is a special enrollment period in which one can sign up for Medicare coverage without penalty.

Part D: Prescription drug coverage

Part D coverage *is not* provided through premiums paid on Parts A and B.

This coverage is offered through private health insurance companies whose plans are priced according to the level of drug coverage desired. The average cost for the Part D plan in 2024 is $59 each month.[12] Medications are ranked in tiers, and many plans offer $0 payment for generic or tier 1 prescriptions. Brand-name and specialty drugs are covered at higher co-pay levels, the cost of which varies from plan to plan. At McIntosh and Associates, we take pride in working with clients to find a prescription drug plan that best deals with their specific medications. We will sort and find cost-effective formulary coverage for you.

As is the case with Part B, there is a late enrollment penalty for Part D coverage. Medicare calculates the penalty by multiplying 1 percent of the "national base beneficiary premium" ($34.70 in 2024) by the number of full, uncovered months you didn't have Part D or creditable coverage.[13] The monthly premium is rounded to the nearest $.10 and added to your monthly Part D premium.

The national base beneficiary premium may change each year, so your penalty amount may also change each year.

I bring this up again mainly because we sometimes encounter people who say, "Well, I don't need Part D coverage because I have no expensive prescriptions right now." They figure they'll add this coverage later when it becomes necessary. That's when I coach them about the lifelong penalty they will pay for every year they could have

---

[12] Medicare. 2024. "What does Medicare cost?" https://www.medicare.gov/basics/get-started-with-medicare/medicare-basics/what-does-medicare-cost#
[13] Medicare. 2024. "Part D late enrollment penalty" https://www.medicare.gov/drug-coverage-part-d/costs-for-medicare-drug-coverage/part-d-late-enrollment-penalty

had Part B or D coverage and declined to take it. Yet I occasionally see people—folks who weren't my clients at age sixty-five—who didn't know the Parts B or D penalties follow them through life. They just assumed it was a one- or two-year penalty. It can be a costly mistake.

Part C: The all-in-one Medicare Advantage package

Part C holds its own unique place under the Medicare coverage and plan selections.

Also known as Medicare Advantage, Part C is essentially an all-in-one package that includes all components of "original Medicare" Parts A and B. In addition, most Advantage plans also include Part D prescription drug coverage along with some add-ons such as an allowance for over-the-counter items like vitamins as well as a fitness club membership, which I am all for! Many Advantage plans also cover preventative services in vision, hearing, and dental care that are not covered by Medicare Parts A and B.

The strongest selling point for Advantage plans is their price, especially when compared to the costs of "Medigap" or Medicare supplemental insurance, described below. Another strong point is the bundle of added benefits and services, items that really increase the total value of your health care coverage. Many Advantage plans can be purchased for little or no cost. (Keep in mind, though, that Advantage participants also must pay the monthly Part B premium.)

Advantage plans are offered by private health insurance companies that essentially administer health care for seniors on Medicare's behalf. Each company in turn receives a monthly fee from Medicare.

The insurance companies attempt to control costs by negotiating prices for fees and services with a network of medical providers—hospitals, physicians, laboratories, urgent care centers, treatment, and rehabilitation centers. Much in the same way that HMOs and PPOs operate, an Advantage participant will typically pay little or nothing to see an in-network primary care physician, and only a co-pay to a network specialist. (Visits to out-of-network providers are permitted, but typically incur a higher cost and sometimes require a pre-visit rereferral.) Fees for hospital stays, medical procedures, and emergency room visits are usually determined in advance.

Most Advantage plans also have a limit on annual out-of-pocket expenses, which offers the consumer many of the same retirement-savings protections as Medicare supplemental insurance. Let's briefly look at the difference between the two.

Medicare Supplement Insurance (aka "Medigap"): Paying for the assurance

Most people know without me having to tell them that Medicare doesn't cover everything. They've heard about the 20 percent of non-hospital costs that are left uncovered by Part B. That may not sound like much until you consider that the average cost of open heart bypass surgery ranges from $30,000 to $200,000.[14] A patient's 20 percent share of those non-hospital charges—the surgeon's fee, the anesthesiologist's fee, the OR assistants, the pre- and post-op medications, and recovery therapy—can easily approach $20,000.

How are you going to pay that bill?

Here is where Medicare supplemental insurance—sometimes called "Medigap coverage"—can make a significant impact on the longevity of any retirement plan.

Medigap plans are individual insurance policies sold by private insurance companies to pay part or all of what Medicare doesn't. The cost of each plan varies depending on the amount of the deductible, the extent of coverage, the health history of the insured, the state of issuance, and other factors. In 2024, the average cost of a Medicare supplemental plan was about $137 a month.[15] That number can

---

[14] Daniel Petkevich. Fair Square. January 27, 2023. "How Much Does Open Heart Surgery Cost with Medicare?" https://fairsquaremedicare.com/articles/how-much-does-open-heart-surgery-cost-with-medicare

[15] Stephanie Guinan. Value Penguin. January 16, 2024. "How Much Does Medicare Cost in 2024?" https://www.valuepenguin.com/medicare-cost#

fluctuate on a variety of factors, including whether you're a man or woman and your place of residence (as determined by your zip code).

Such a plan can be well worth the cost for some people.

Let's say you are about to turn sixty-five and are considering all your Medicare options. Your body is telling you (and your orthopedist agrees) that you've got a hip replacement looming in your immediate future. Or maybe you need ongoing dialysis or radiation/chemo treatments in a fight against cancer. People who know they will soon need some costly medical attention would do well to consider supplemental coverage.

I pray that none of this applies to you. But if these or any other ongoing medical treatments are a part of your life, the money you spend on Medigap coverage might save you from spending additional retirement dollars on out-of-pocket expenses not covered by Medicare Part B.

Here is where we work closely with clients to select an appropriate supplemental plan, as not all are created equal.

Plans are identified from letters A through N, and some cover more—and consequently cost more—than others. In 2024, Plans G and N were generally regarded as providing the most coverage[16], and they are the plans I recommend to roughly nine of ten people facing significant medical expenses in retirement. But the picture is continually changing. Plan F, for example, was once considered the gold standard but is no longer available to new enrollees. This is why you need an insurance professional, such as myself or a member of my team, by your side when you sort out these often-complicated decisions.

For other people, however, there is a less costly alternative to consider.

You likely won't hear this from many other people in the financial services industry—many of whom, frankly, would rather talk about anything but health insurance—but we often find ourselves

---

[16] Boomer Benefits. 2024. "Plan G vs. Plan N: The Best Medicare Supplement Plan" https://boomerbenefits.com/plan-g-vs-plan-n-the-best-medicare-supplement-plan/

recommending lower premium Advantage plans to many of our clients seeking ways to control the rising cost of health care in retirement.

The reasons for doing so seem obvious. Advantage plans can be purchased for considerably less than supplemental policies. Some plans, in fact, carry a $0 premium. People in reasonably good health and whose medical providers are within a growing network of Advantage companies can often save money—money they can spend on other needs or wants in retirement—by considering an Advantage plan over a Medicare supplement.

We know people, for instance, who are receiving income only from Social Security, and maybe an annuity payment. For some of these folks, their health insurance premiums are almost more than they can handle. Moving them to an Advantage plan often removes some of the pressure they feel in paying health care premiums.

But there's also a less-obvious reason for recommending Advantage plans, one that shows up when taking a closer look under the hood.

What happens, you might ask, if I later develop a medical condition that requires more costly care? Would an Advantage plan protect me from potential devastating costs? It's a great question, and one that merits a closer look.

My response would be to point out that even in a worst-case situation, the annual Advantage cap on out-of-pocket expenses is often less than one pays each year for premiums on a full-coverage supplemental plan. A couple, for example, might find themselves paying $4,000 or more a year in supplemental premiums while their out-of-pocket limit under an Advantage plan is only $3,800. It's why we're seeing more people move over to Advantage plans as they get older.

I'd also point out that no Medigap decision is written in stone. People have the option to change coverage during the open enrollment period that begins each October—a period greeted by a seemingly never-ending stream of TV ads for Advantage programs. (For the record, the ads run way too many times, and you need to be cautious as to whom you give information. Still, I rather appreciate the coverage Advantage plans can provide.)

Advantage plans also can be an option for folks who have saved into a Health Savings Account (HSA) and have those funds available to buffer any unexpected out-of-pocket medical costs. For these people, using an Advantage plan can be a great opportunity for cost, coverage, and peace of mind.

Bottom line: Advantage plans save money on premiums upfront, but you may have greater on-going costs if you need extensive services. And when you consider inflation and the rising costs of health care, that's money that might be redirected toward spending somewhere else if you're relatively healthy. It can be very helpful.

Hedging investments to pay for health care: The Fixed Index Annuity and Health Savings Account

Let's conclude this look at covering health care in retirement by looking at some alternate ways to pay for it.

Even with insurance coverage, the costs of prescription drugs—especially when dealing with cancer or other chronic diseases—can be staggering. This is why we occasionally develop a potential stream of regular income designated exclusively to help pay these or other medical expenses.

We'll talk in the next chapter about the income-producing ability of the fixed indexed annuity (FIA). But for now, let's just note that we sometimes encourage clients to consider this insurance-backed product that in time can produce regular income that can be used for any need, including prescription drug costs, insurance premiums, co-pays, and other out-of-pocket medical costs. Some offer the ability for the annuity payments to be adjusted for inflation, thus providing a hedge against rising health care costs. We'll also talk in a later chapter about using annuity options as a source for helping to pay for long-term nursing care.

Finally, don't overlook—as too many people do, sadly—the advantages of the Health Savings Account (HSA).

The IRS tax code allows HSA contributions to be made by people who have a "high-deductible health plan," which is defined as one having more than a $4,000 annual deductible. Tax-deferred contributions can be made up to a limit that changes each year. In 2024, that limit is $4,150 for an individual account and $8,300 for a family plan.[17] Contributions, which can be made by an employer or employee, do not count as taxable income in the year they are made. Moreover, distributions from the fund are not taxed when used for qualified health care purposes. Among those are paying COBRA premiums, meeting deductibles, and paying for long-term care. You should be aware there are penalties for withdrawing money from an HSA for nonqualified, non-medical reasons.

The beauty of the HSA, in my opinion, is its versatility. Money in the account can be invested and grown tax-free, and I believe the account realizes its greatest potential when developed in this manner. Contributions cannot be made after reaching Medicare age at sixty-five, but assets in the fund can continue to grow and be used long after that. Be sure to review the options and try to have the account invested into funds for growth as your risk tolerance allows. You don't want to have your money just sitting idly in an account with little to no growth generated.

Building up a pool of health care money just makes sense to me. That's why I often encourage many clients who are under sixty-five and still working, whether self-employed or otherwise, to consider contributing to a Health Savings Account. It could be a great way of hedging money against taxes, both when contributions are made and later when money can be taken tax-free from the account if needed for qualified medical purposes. We're a big proponent of HSAs and several other ways to save money that can eventually pay for this potentially significant drain on a retirement nest egg.

---

[17] Voya Financial. December 11, 2023. "How much can you contribute to your HAS and FSA in 2024?" https://www.voya.com/blog/how-much-can-you-contribute-to-your-hsa-and-fsa-2024#

CHAPTER 4

Strategies: Planning for Lifelong Income

A concern we hear most from clients is, "Will I run out of money in retirement?" People are understandably concerned about living longer than their money does.

Well, you're right to be concerned. For you are about to enter a new phase of life, a transition from years of earning steady wages and accumulating wealth into a time of having to take income—hard, cold cash—from those assets you've saved. This is the time you go from thinking about putting away money for retirement and instead consider ways to take distributions from those savings while trying to make them last for however long you might live.

This transition is easier said than done.

You will never hear me suggest that life is easy—I've already told you of my family's financial struggles in my younger years—but some times are more cut-and-dried than others. During our working years, for instance, we collect regular paychecks and pay recurring expenses. We pay monthly utility bills, buy groceries, put new shoes on the ever-growing feet of our kids, make mortgage and car loan payments. We set aside money for vacations and recreational/entertainment activities. Many of us set up a college fund for the kids. And when we need additional money, we can always work overtime, get a promotion or seek employment in a second job. These are the typical adjustments we make when we need to make ends meet.

But things are greatly different in retirement.

Now suddenly we must provide our own paychecks to pay for many of the same expenses we knew earlier in life. True, the kids no longer need new shoes or college money. But other expenses rise up in their place, especially as our bodies wear down and require more medical attention. And now when additional income is needed—such as when unchecked inflation suddenly reappears—we may find ourselves with few readily available income-expanding options beyond annual Social Security cost of living adjustments (COLAs, which <u>in reality, do not tend to keep pace with inflation</u>).

Providing our own income in retirement is not a simple matter and involves multiple items to address. Among the many:

When do you hope to retire? Do you plan to take Social Security at age sixty-two, your earliest opportunity, or wait until Full Retirement Age (FRA), or even later? (This decision, as we will soon see, can make a significant impact on the baseline Social Security benefit you will receive for the rest of your life.)

What other sources of reliable, "fixed" income can you count on other than Social Security? Are you one of the lucky people who will still receive a pension? Will you have rental or farm-related income? Will you have any guaranteed annuity payments? Do you envision working on a part-time basis after stepping away from the everyday workforce?

Which of your retirement savings accounts will you tap first when extra income is needed? Your savings account? Your tax-deferred accounts such as your IRA or 401(k), or your tax-free Roth IRA? And, once again and perhaps most importantly, how can you make sure this money will be available for twenty, thirty, or even more years of retirement?

These considerations are all part of the essential planning needed to guarantee that regular sources of income will last as long as you (and a spouse) do.

Here is where it is especially important to have a financial professional help guide you into this new phase of life. Here is where the work we did in our FOCUS phase—our examination of your possible longevity, your history of saving and investments, what you typically spend each month now, and what you might expect to spend in retirement—comes into play. Here is where we work to determine how much income you might need in retirement, both in the near- and long-term future. Here is where we show you how that income can be produced, and equally important, how long it should last.

This is why income planning is Strategy No. 2 on our list of tools we use to develop a FOCUS Wealth Plan.

What exactly is income planning?

Income planning begins with an informed estimation of what you will spend each month, both now and later in life, on both essential and discretionary expenses—aka, the "fun things in life" that you've earned the chance to enjoy. We then compare those estimates to what you will receive in dependable "fixed" income, the primary source of which is Social Security for most people in retirement. We then add in other reliable income sources—pension or annuity payments, rental or farm income, dividend and interest income, wages from regular or self-employment—then compare the two estimates.

Don't be surprised if, initially at least, what's going out is greater than what's coming in. This is commonly called the "income gap," and our job now is to help you fill it.

We typically do so from the assets you've spent a lifetime saving in what most people call their "retirement nest egg." This often is money you've invested in a tax-deferred IRA or 401(k), or money that's already been taxed and is growing in a brokerage account or a tax-free Roth IRA.

The challenge in retirement is to strategically choose how and when to take money from these different sources. What accounts do we tap first? What accounts do we continue to grow for later use? Which accounts can be tapped in a tax-advantageous way?

Here is where my team can help you in a tough decision-making process. Here is where we can examine which assets are growing better than others—the fruit ready to pick as opposed to that which needs further ripening. Here is where we can talk about how much you might take annually in order to help preserve your nest egg for a lifetime. Here is where we can consider alternative ways of developing other reliable income streams, often using insurance products that we'll discuss here shortly.

And most importantly, here is where we spell out a plan that details exactly where your monthly income will come from, and how much it could be. This will be a plan with contingencies for emergencies, that features strategies for dealing with taxes and offers the potential for continued growth. This plan also will detail how income will continue to be produced for a spouse or other loved ones when we are no longer here.

Moreover, this will be a written plan, one that can be easily understood by an individual or both spouses. The key words in the above sentence are "written" and "easily understood."

Look, I don't believe in presenting a thirty-two-page plan with tons of illustrations that no one will read. But I do believe in the importance of having a written plan that details your financial future in retirement. Here are my expenses. Here are my assets. Here is what I can expect to draw in guaranteed income this year, next year, three, five, and ten years from now. Here is how I expect to fill the income gap from my savings and investments, and here is how I will make sure I don't outlive those assets. Here is how my family will be protected whether I live a long time or pass sooner than expected. And finally, here is verification that I have the means to support myself (and/or a spouse) for as long as we both shall live.

This plan also will be flexible. We will monitor it continually and make adjustments when necessary. But that's a subject for a future chapter.

Don't overlook inflation

This income plan also will make adjustments for inflation, which has always been a factor in planning even when it was relatively tame in the first twenty years of the current century. As measured by the Consumer Price Index, annual inflation was 2.0 percent or lower eight times in twelve years from 2009 (the year after The Great Recession) though 2020. (Contrast that to a period from 1969 through 1982 when annual inflation topped 5.5 percent twelve times in a fourteen-year period, with double-digit inflation in four of those years.)[18]

But inflation became worrisome once again in the emergence from the COVID-19 pandemic. Beginning around mid-2021, Americans coming out of quarantine and isolation suddenly seemed eager to spend money on goods and services that now were in short supply, partly the result of production slowdowns/shutdowns and breaks in the supply chain. More money chasing fewer goods and services is the classic formula for inflation.

By June 2022, year-over-year inflation was 9.1 percent, the highest monthly increase in forty years.[19] That March, the Russian invasion of Ukraine and the resulting economic sanctions, including a boycott of Russian oil, triggered a dramatic increase in gasoline price at the pump. With rising prices in food and fuel, many Americans felt inflation's true pinch for the first time in their lives.

Bottom line, your dollar in 2022 wasn't buying as much as it did just a year earlier. As of the start of 2023, the inflation rate was still hovering

---

[18] U.S. Inflation Calculator. 2024. "Historical Inflation Rates: 1914-2024"
https://www.usinflationcalculator.com/inflation/historical-inflation-rates/
[19] U.S. Bureau of Labor Statistics. July 18, 2022. "Consumer prices up 9.1 percent over the year ended June 2022, largest increase in 40 years"
https://www.bls.gov/opub/ted/2022/consumer-prices-up-9-1-percent-over-the-year-ended-june-2022-largest-increase-in-40-years.htm

above 6.5 percent, though by October 2024, the inflation rated had dropped to 2.5 percent—its lowest mark since February 2021.[20][21]

Again, there's always been a need to adjust for inflation in any income plan, but that need is even more pressing now. Rather than having people living a lesser lifestyle than they envisioned, it becomes increasingly important to find ways of increasing income as inflation rises. A person nearing or actually into retirement needs to know not only what their income will look like today, but also two years, five years, ten years, and twenty years down the road.

Social Security

Helping clients make a Social Security decision that's right for them is one of the most important things we do. I say this because:

1) Social Security is the primary source of guaranteed income for most older Americans. Of the 65 million Americans on Social Security in 2021, the U.S. Census Bureau estimates that half of them receive 50 percent or more of their monthly income from the program. Moreover, about one in seven older Americans receive 90 percent of all income from Social Security.[22]

2) The decision you make when first taking Social Security establishes a monthly benefit amount that stays with you for the rest of your life. This initial benefit value also affects spousal and survivor benefits, which we'll explain here shortly.

There are people who offer "conventional wisdom" on the best time to begin taking Social Security. That advice typically involves "maximizing" one's benefits by not taking them until they top out at age

---

[20] Y Charts. August 2024. "US Inflation Rate" https://ycharts.com/indicators/us_inflation_rate

[21] Sarah Foster. Bankrate. September 11, 2024. "Inflation continues to cool but some items are still pricey — here's what's rising most" https://www.bankrate.com/banking/federal-reserve/latest-inflation-statistics/#:

[22] Center for Budget and Policy Priorities. May 31, 2024. "Policy Basics: Top Ten Facts about Social Security" https://www.cbpp.org/research/social-security/top-ten-facts-about-social-security

seventy. It's hard to argue with that—if, that is, you have income sources other than Social Security to carry you through to age seventy.

But not everyone has this luxury. Many people find themselves needing their benefits at their earliest possible time (as soon as age sixty-two), or can only wait until full retirement age (either sixty-six or sixty-seven for most readers of this book). So, I'm not going to make any blanket recommendations here. I wouldn't do so, anyway, without first knowing more about your unique situation. To do that, I'd need answers to questions like:

What would make you want to retire early if you could? Has your work situation come to the point that you simply have to get away? Are you stepping away whether you want to or not? Are there other conditions, such as your own health considerations or needing to care for a loved one, that might force you into early retirement, which we'll define here as any departure from the workforce before reaching full retirement age (FRA)? Is your plan to travel the world or enjoy the simple things in life that time would give you?

Other questions to consider:

If you do retire early, how will you support yourself? Will you need to turn on your Social Security benefits early, knowing that if you do, you will receive a reduced monthly benefit (when compared to what you would have received at FRA) for the rest of your life? Or, are there other means available by which you can support yourself or your family until you reach FRA?

Does your early retirement plan include any kind of continued employment? If so, we need to look at how your already reduced monthly benefit might be lowered even more by a Social Security "takeback" that occurs when wages earned while receiving benefits before reaching FRA exceed a certain threshold. We'll look more at this "earnings test" in our next chapter on taxes, but for now, it's important to consider how this further reduction in a monthly benefit might affect your income plan.

And finally, might you be in a position to defer starting Social Security until after FRA? We're talking here about taking advantage of *delayed retirement credits* that increase a monthly benefit by about 8 percent for each full year in which Social Security start-up is delayed between FRA and age seventy when the delayed credits end.

But again, we're getting a bit ahead of ourselves. We need to look first at some Social Security basics, things some people know but are the subject of many questions we hear.

First, who qualifies for the program? Most American workers do, but not everyone. You qualify upon earning forty "work credits." In 2024, a worker received a credit after earning wages of $1,730 in each quarter of the year.[23] Most Americans earn four credits a year, meaning a ten-year work history—though not necessarily ten consecutive years—will qualify one for Social Security.

Second, the full monthly benefit to which you are entitled depends on how much you paid into your personal account through Social Security taxes withheld from your paycheck throughout your working career. There is a limit on how much of your earnings can be taxed in a single year ($168,200 in 2024)[24], as well as the maximum monthly benefit you can receive ($3,822 in 2024 for a person starting benefits at FRA).[25]

Third, the full benefit to which you are entitled is payable upon reaching your full retirement age, which varies slightly for people of different ages. The following chart breaks it down.

---

[23] Social Security. 2024. "Latest amount & QC explanation" https://www.ssa.gov/oact/cola/QC.html

[24] Social Security. 2024. "Contribution And Benefit Base" https://www.ssa.gov/oact/cola/cbb.html

[25] Social Security. January 2, 2024. "What is the maximum Social Security retirement benefit payable?" https://faq.ssa.gov/en-US/Topic/article/KA-01897

Age to Receive Full Social Security Benefits*

(Called "full retirement age" [FRA] or "normal retirement age.")

Year of Birth*	FRA
1943-1954	66
1955	66 and 2 months
1956	66 and 4 months
1957	66 and 6 months
1958	66 and 8 months
1959	66 and 10 months
1960 and later	67

*If you were born on Jan. 1 of any year, you should refer to the previous year. (If you were born on the 1st of the month, we figure your benefit [and your full retirement age] as if your birthday was in the previous month.)

Fourth, the amount of the monthly benefit you receive depends on when you first begin taking it. Moreover, that first benefit sets a payment baseline that follows you throughout life and is adjusted upward only by cost-of-living adjustments (COLAs) determined by the Social Security Administration (SSA).

Benefits started before reaching FRA are permanently reduced by about 6 percent (or slightly more) for each full year between starting time and FRA. The theory here is that because you'll be receiving more payments over the course of your life, you will receive less money in each payment.

The chart below shows the effect on a $1,000 hypothetical monthly benefit if taken early by people of various ages.

Benefit Reduction When First Taken at Age 62[26]

Year of birth	Months between age 62 and FRA	$1,000 monthly reduced to:	$500 spouse benefit reduced to:
1943-1954	48	$750 (-25%)	$350 (-30%)
1955	50	$741 (-25.83%)	$345 (-30.83%)
1956	52	$733 (-26.67%)	$341 (-31.67%)
1957	54	$725 (-27.5%)	$337 (-32.5%)
1958	56	$716 (-28.33%)	333 (-33.3%)
1959	58	$708 (-29.17%)	$329 (-34.17%)
1960	60	$700 (-30.0%)	$325 (-35.05)

Conversely, your monthly benefit can be permanently *increased* when delaying start-up until after FRA. Delayed retirement credits will increase a benefit by 8 percent for each full year between FRA and start-up time. These delayed credits end at age seventy.

Fifth and final note. The benefit you establish upon first taking payments also affects the benefit available to a spouse who lacks their own qualifying work history. The same applies to a widow or widower of a qualifying worker. Let's look at that briefly.

Social Security provides a benefit for a spouse who does not qualify through their own work history. Such a person, such as a stay-at-home parent whose hard work is not rewarded in "work credits," can receive up to half of a qualifying spouse's monthly benefit. Again, the benefit established by the qualifying spouse sets the standard for the spousal benefit, which also is affected by whether the spousal benefit is taken

---

[26] Social Security Administration. 2024. "Starting Your Retirement Benefits Early" https://www.ssa.gov/benefits/retirement/planner/agereduction.html

before or at FRA. Note that a spouse whose work history qualifies for benefits will automatically receive the larger of either the spousal benefit or their own work-history benefit.

Benefits also are available to surviving spouses.

In most cases, survivor benefits become available at age sixty, though one can receive them at age fifty (if disabled) or even earlier when caring for dependent children of the deceased. If both spouses were receiving benefits, the survivor receives the higher benefit of the two upon the death of the other. The other benefit disappears. But here again, the amount of the benefit being taken by one spouse affects what is available to the other.

Clearly, there are more elements of Social Security than I can detail in one section of one chapter. I've not, for example, described the disability aspect of the program, choosing instead to concentrate on the retirement-age benefits. We also didn't discuss spousal or survivor benefits for divorced people. But I'll be glad to answer any questions you have—and people have plenty—in helping guide you to Social Security decisions that are right for you.

Pensions, or pension-like income

Pensions, once considered one of the essential legs of the "retirement stool," are becoming increasingly rare today. Employer-sponsored pensions, once regarded as one of the "defined benefits" of employment, have been replaced over time by "defined contributions" plans. These put the onus on employees to fund their own pensions (along with smaller contributions from employers). Hence, the emphasis today is on the 401(k), 403(b)s, and other employee-based retirement plans.

But the traditional pension isn't extinct just yet. Many employees of government agencies still receive one or are promised one. Some larger private companies still offer them, and I'm happy for anyone still fortunate enough to receive one.

The lucky few, however, have some choices to make regarding how they receive their pension payments when retirement finally comes.

Some have the option to take a lump-sum payment. Others have options to receive annuity payments throughout their lifetime, with the payments expiring when they do. Others might opt for a slightly lower monthly payment that covers not only their lifetime but also that of a spouse. Some wanting the assurance of payments in the event of an untimely passing might opt for "period certain" payments of ten to twenty years. This way, somebody you love is assured of receiving payments over a defined period of time, even if it's not you.

So many choices, so many questions.

Again, here is where we stand ready with answers and options. Not just on matters of pension distributions, but also on other issues of immediate versus long-term payment opportunities. We might consider, for instance, those from an insurance settlement, an early retirement or contract buyout, the sale of property or a business interest, an inheritance, or—in your dreams—a lottery winning. (No, we don't see many of those, darn the luck.)

When reviewing our clients' pension options, we often encourage them to take a lump-sum distribution that they immediately roll over into an IRA. By doing so, a pensioner (as opposed to their employer) takes control of the money—how it is invested and grown, how much and when it can be withdrawn at any time. Better yet, the pensioner now has this money in hand and avoids the possibility that a financially strapped government body or business suddenly decides to limit—or cut completely—future pension payments. Believe me, that's an important consideration in today's world of often- underfunded pension funds.

Also, with more control over how this money is invested—using options not always available in a company-controlled pension—we might diversify. Or, we might use that lump sum of money to create a new stream of guaranteed income from, for instance, an annuity whose regular payments might be used for health care or prescription drug expenses.

This is another way of helping to ensure that your regular expenses can be met every single month. We generally want to address as much of those recurring monthly expenses as we can with sustainable, reliable income—Social Security, a pension, an annuity payment—before we start taking income from market-risk investments that may be up or down on any given day.

Let's look at another way of producing this kind of regular income.

Annuities

I'm an unabashed believer in the income-producing reliability of an annuity, an insurance product whose ability to make payments is backed by the claims-paying ability of an insurance company.

OK, I hear you.

Many people hear the word "annuity" and immediately think, "run." They've been warned by Susie Orman and others to be careful about annuities. And yes, there are some annuity products that are better suited to those in their early earning years who can afford to take a riskier approach with their assets. Orman and others are usually talking about the **variable annuity,** a product that often involves a higher fee structure and account values that rise and fall daily with the ebb and flow of the stock market.

No, I don't like those either for those who are nearing retirement and can't stomach market volatility. There are, in my opinion, better annuity options—among them the **fixed annuity** that pays a fixed rate of interest. A fixed annuity in 2024 might generate interest of around 4 percent, which is keeping pace with declining inflation rates.[27]

I'm more inclined to recommend the *fixed index annuity* (FIA) where appropriate: it's an insurance contract that offers an annuitant the chance for growth potential through a limited share of "credited interest" based on a potential increase in an external market index (S&P 500, Dow Jones Industrial Average, etc.). As a tradeoff for getting only a capped part or limited participation (say, 50 percent) in that growth— a ceiling, if you will—an FIA also has a floor that protects against losses due to market performance. The insurance company (as opposed to the

---

[27] Jennifer Schell. Annuity.org. September 26, 2024. "Are Annuity Rates Going Up?" https://www.annuity.org/annuities/rates/cost-of-waiting/

investor) assumes the risk against losses. This floor is typically zero, which means that there may be years when the FIA earns no interest, but you don't lose any interest already credited due to market declines.

The FIA may also offer a level of tax efficiency. When you're not taking income from the account, it has the potential to grow tax-deferred. For accounts funded with after-tax dollars—"non-qualified" money in IRS terms—you pay tax only on the interest growth of any money you take out of the account. Withdrawals are subject to taxes only when withdrawn, although you will pay a 10 percent federal penalty for withdrawals before age fifty-nine and a half.

The FIA also has flexibility you can use as market conditions change. You can change how your premiums are allocated within the contract, too. But the bottom line is that the FIA is a long-term retirement income vehicle that can guarantee income payments for life while protecting against market volatility.

The living benefits of life insurance

A lot of people approaching retirement age hear the words "life insurance" and immediately say, "Ahh, I'm good, thanks. I mean, why do I need life insurance at this later stage in my life?"

Again, I hear you. But we often find ourselves advising people to take a new look on life. Specifically, to take a new look at today's life insurance products, many of which have benefits beyond those of policies sold to your parents and grandparents.

To be sure, the traditional reason for purchasing life insurance has always been, and remains today, securing a death benefit that financially protects loved ones and other beneficiaries following the untimely demise of the insured. But many of today's whole life policies—as opposed to term life coverage—also have benefits you can use while still living. For people who can qualify medically and financially, whole life insurance can provide some financial flexibility through policy loans that can be used for college expenses, a first-time home purchase or future medical or long-term care needs. And like most life insurance, they involve fees and charges, including potential surrender penalties for withdrawals.

You may, for instance, be able to use *indexed universal life insurance* (IUL) to take retirement income that can be available tax-free. You read that right. For just as IRS rules allow the death benefit of an insurance policy to be received tax-free by beneficiaries, so too do those rules also allow the insured to receive tax-free payments from the policy while still alive. Let's look at how these "living benefits" work.

Insurance such as the IUL allows the insured to take tax-free income via loans taken against the policy's cash value, which is typically grown through investment strategies of the issuing insurance company. Not to get too technical here, but the IRS treats a loan differently than it does an ordinary taxable distribution. The insured can thus secure a tax-free loan by essentially borrowing from themselves. They then have the option of repaying the loan over time at an interest rate that is typically lower than that on a conventional bank loan.

Or, the insured can choose not to repay the loan. In this option, the loan value decreases both the cash value and the death benefit on the policy. We strongly urge people to do this only with the guidance of an insurance professional (such as a member of my team), as a policy can lapse or require additional premiums should a cash value fall to $0.[28]

The IUL has another important "living benefit" to consider.

We'll discuss funding for long-term care (LTC) in much more detail in a later chapter. But for now, let's note here that many IUL policies make money available for essential nursing care. Many have provisions you can purchase that allow the use of up to 50 percent of the death benefit for LTC when the insured cannot meet two of the six activities of daily living (ADL), which we'll define later. If you never use this source for LTC—and I sincerely hope you don't have to—you still have the full death benefit available for loved ones. Beyond that, you will not

---

[28] Policy loans and withdrawals will reduce available cash values and death benefits and may cause the policy to lapse or affect any guarantees against lapse. Additional premium payments may be required to keep the policy in force. In the event of a lapse, outstanding policy loans in excess of unrecovered cost basis will be subject to ordinary income tax. Tax laws are subject to change. You should consult a tax professional.

have spent additional money on a traditional "use it or lose it" LTC policy.

The ability to use the benefits of today's life insurance while you're still here to do so is a major reason we urge clients to take a "second look" at a concept they might not otherwise consider.

Today's whole life policies can meet a variety of retirement preparation needs. One policy doesn't allow every feature to be exercised—by exercising one feature, you reduce the value of another—yet the options allow you to choose the benefits that best meet your situation. Provide additional sources of income: Check. Provide a source of funding for possible long-term care: Check. Provide tax-free income, both for yourself and/or loved ones: Check. Develop flexibility in how and when you take additional income as conditions change: Check. Provide a hedge against inflation: Check.

With these types of policies, you feel more like you are in the driver's seat, and—to steal a line from a GM advertising campaign—you're no longer driving our parents' Buick.

Other income alternatives

We also welcome the opportunity to explore other income sources with our clients.

Many people as younger investors routinely reinvested stock dividends or interest from bonds. It's a sound investment strategy. But now as retirement approaches, perhaps it's time we consider taking those dividends and interest as income, especially if taken from non-qualified accounts that get more favorable tax treatment. (More on that in the next chapter.)

Here in central Michigan, we often find people looking at potential income from the rental of farmland. Long-time, hard-working farmers who no longer want to toil as hard as they once did might rent some of their property to a younger farmer. (I have some experience in this matter, having watched both the hard work and the eventual transition during my younger years.)

We're also seeing a somewhat new trend here in which people are renting their land to companies that harness wind energy. We can help landowners develop alternative streams of income here as well.

We'll also consider different strategies that might be used when taking income from retirement savings.

You will ideally have money invested in different "tax buckets," which we'll describe in more detail in our next chapter on taxes in retirement. A key part of income planning is considering tax implications when taking income, as every dollar paid in taxes is one less dollar you have available to spend. So here is where we will look at how additional income might affect your tax picture. Are you better off taking income from taxable brokerage accounts, or from tax-deferred accounts? Do we need to look to money from tax-free sources, or can we let those accounts continue to grow?

How will current marginal tax rates affect your decisions? At the time of the writing of this book, tax rates—believe it or not—were at some of the lowest levels in some forty years. If you have money (and you likely do) in tax-deferred accounts such as an IRA or 401(k), here is a time to consider moving money out of those accounts, either for income or as part of a tax conversion strategy and paying the mandatory tax on the withdrawals when rates are relatively low. Again, we'll look more closely at tax strategies in the next chapter.

We'll also look at current market conditions before taking income from at-risk retirement savings.

Which of your investment assets are up in value and might have profits we can tap? Which are underperforming and need time to recover? Knowing when to harvest your crop and when to let it develop further—to use a farming analogy from my youth—is a big part of assuring the longevity of your retirement nest egg.

Employment during retirement

And finally, let's not forget the prospect of employment in retirement. (Notice I didn't say "working in retirement," as I happen to believe that we're always "working" at something, even if not for wages, on a daily basis.)

Look, I would never discourage anyone who *wants* to work. I've been around hard-working people all my life, and I'm better off for it. But a slightly different standard should apply in retirement.

This is a time when people should work only because they *like* to do so as opposed to because they *need* to do so. If you enjoy working part-time in either your former or a new position, perhaps as a way of easing into retirement or staying close to people whose company you enjoy, then hooray for you. Business owners might reduce their daily hours but remain involved in a venture they helped build. People with valuable expertise may be encouraged to stay on in a consultancy role. A skilled worker might consider picking up a few hours here or there. Whatever your reason for doing so, staying active in retirement is always a positive thing.

And hey, the additional income often comes in handy as well.

But again, the motivation in doing this should be because you *want* to do it. I don't want any person in retirement to feel *obligated* to work in order to make ends meet, or to feel like they can't care for an elderly parent because they're still working nine to five. If you find yourself in that situation, let's talk about adjustments that could make a difference in your future.

CHAPTER 5

Strategies: Reduce the Bite of Taxes

I've yet to meet anyone who likes paying taxes. True, I know some people who pay their taxes with less grumbling than others, but I've yet to find anyone who looks forward to it. I seriously doubt that you know such a person, either.

Having said that, however, let's also acknowledge that there are times when meeting our tax obligations is easier than others.

In our working years, for instance, we typically have taxes taken from our regular paychecks through a withholding process. This is money we literally never see. We know it's disappearing gradually, but we often don't appreciate the extent of it until April rolls around and we are required to report how much we've actually paid in taxes over the previous year. If we didn't pay enough, we are required to pay more, which really causes us to grumble. If we paid too much, we get a refund and our discontent subsides, slightly, for another year.

But things are a little different in retirement. Without regular paychecks, there is often no regular withholding. Consequently, we often see our tax payments flying out the window in big chunks, either as estimated payments on a quarterly basis, or in a large lump sum at tax reporting time in April.

Taxes seem to take a bigger bite from our bottom (lines) at these times.

Retirement also presents some unique tax situations we've not encountered in our working years. At the head of the list: That pool of tax-deferred money we've spent years of accumulating in IRAs, 401(k)s, 403(b)s, and others of what the IRS calls "qualified" retirement savings programs suddenly arrives with a tax bill. At age seventy-three, we are required to begin taking money out of those accounts—whether we actually need it or not—and pay tax on the distributions. (Prior to the passing of SECURE Act 2.0 in 2022, the age was seventy-two. By the year 2033, the age will inch up to seventy-five.) This money not only presents an immediate new tax bill, but also could potentially elevate us into a higher tax bracket, perhaps even one higher than we knew in our working years.

This possibility is a contradiction of what we were told was likely to happen when we first started putting money into tax-deferred accounts.

The well-intended advice then was that we would receive less income, and consequently be in a lower tax bracket, when it came time to pay tax on this money in retirement. Nice theory, but in reality, most people hope to avoid a reduced standard of living in retirement and are often surprised to find that their income, as well as their income tax, does not change considerably.

This surprise can be illustrated by a call I got from a client anxious to vent. "Wow," she said, "I never would have imagined that I would pay more taxes in Year One of retirement than I did in my highest earning year while working."

Well, having wealth and reliable income is hardly a bad situation, but it can result in higher taxes when that income is produced from tax-deferred accounts with a high balance. We immediately began working with this person to start reducing the amount in her tax-deferred pool by moving money into more tax-efficient vehicles that can help reduce her tax bill. We also began coaching her and some younger family members to consider building up a bucket of tax-free savings at a younger age.

Other retirement-age taxes kick in as well. Social Security can be taxed, which surprises some people who note—accurately—that they've been paying a Social Security tax throughout their working lives. Well, they did, but that tax was used to fund the program. Now they also might have to pay a tax on its benefits. More on this is coming later in the chapter.

Higher earners also might be looking at an additional surcharge on monthly Medicare Part B premiums. This is not technically a tax, I guess, but anytime the government increases a cost, it sure feels like a tax to me.

Similarly, an earnings test on wages earned while taking Social Security benefits before reaching full retirement age (FRA) isn't technically a tax. But when the government is taking money out of your benefits—and directly out of your pocket—it sure feels and smells like a tax.

And now for the really scary part, an acknowledgement of the monster we all know is in the room.

These taxes are likely only going to increase in the future. That's why now is the time to let us help you develop a plan to help reduce your future taxes. The goal in doing so is to retain more of your money, actual cash you can spend on either the necessary expenses of life or the bucket-list experiences you've been dreaming of providing for yourself or loved ones.

The prospect of future higher taxes

This is why my team at McIntosh and Associates puts such special emphasis on tax strategies in our FOCUS Wealth Plan.

To me, a big part of any retirement plan involves keeping as much of *your* money in *your* pocket instead of paying it to the IRS. When you're fighting for every dollar you need for yourself and your family in retirement, you should fight to keep every dollar you legally and morally don't have to pay your Uncle Sam. This is why, in my opinion, tax planning has replaced traditional concepts of asset allocation and growth as a leading component of retirement planning.

The need for this planning becomes especially acute when taking the long-range view of future taxation in our country.

Does anyone truly believe taxes are going down in the near future? I sincerely doubt it, especially when remembering that we already saw a significant tax cut at the start of 2018. Yes, you read that correctly. That's when the Tax Cuts and Jobs Act—aka, the Trump tax cuts—took effect and reduced marginal tax rates to their lowest levels in some forty years. (See chart below.) But these reduced rates are scheduled to "sunset" at the start of 2026, and most people believe that higher rates will follow.

IRS Tax Brackets, Then and Now

Single Filer			
2017[29]		2024[30]	
10%	$0-$9,325	10%	$0-$11,600
15%	$9,326-$37,950	12%	$11,601-$47,150
25%	$37,951-$91,900	22%	$47,151-$100,525
28%	$91,901-$191,650	24%	$100,526-$191,950
33%	$191,651-$416,700	32%	$191,951-$243,725
35%	$416,701-$418,400	35%	$243,726-$609,350
39.6%	Over $418,401	37%	Over $609,351

---

[29] Bankrate. November 28, 2018. "2017 tax bracket rates" https://www.bankrate.com/taxes/2017-tax-brackets
[30] Sabrina Parys. NerdWallet. May 30, 2024. "2024 Tax Brackets and Federal Income Tax Rates" https://www.nerdwallet.com/article/taxes/federal-income-tax-brackets

Married Filing Jointly			
2017		2024	
10%	$0-$18,650	10%	$0-$23,200
15%	$18,651-$75,900	12%	$23,201-$94,300
25%	$75,901-$153,100	22%	$94,301-$201,050
28%	$153,101-$233,350	24%	$201,051-$383,900
33%	$233,351-$416,700	32%	$383,901-$487,450
35%	$416,701-$470,700	35%	$487,451-$731,200
39.6%	Over $470,701	37%	Over $731,201

Yes, rub those eyes and look again. Tax rates are lower today (in 2023) than they were just six years ago. But again, the key question is how long they might remain this low.

Now let's consider the effect of our ever-increasing national debt and the role taxes will likely play toward paying it off.

The economic uncertainty brought about by the COVID-19 pandemic only increased this debt. Relief spending designed to help Americans weather layoffs—either temporary or permanent because of COVID-related quarantines and business shutdowns—was appreciated but arrived at a cost of trillions in additional debt. Post-pandemic inflation and rising health care costs that increased Medicare spending also contributed to the rising debt, as did the reduced tax collections that accompanied the 2018 reduction in tax brackets. Tax collections were further reduced in post-pandemic America when laid-off workers suddenly became reluctant to return to their former positions. Having 5 million more job openings than people in the U.S. is hardly a way of reducing national debt through higher tax collections.[31]

(OK, that last comment is a personal observation rooted in my rural Michigan upbringing. I won't take it back. My father always told me to work hard and do the right thing. He talked often about the importance of honesty, integrity, and being humble. A dirty face at the end of a long

---

[31] Jeff Cox. CNBC. March 29, 2022. "There are now a record 5 million more job openings than unemployed people in the U.S." https://www.cnbc.com/2022/03/29/there-are-now-a-record-5-million-more-job-openings-than-unemployed-people-in-the-us.html

day was evidence of his willingness to meet a challenge, and proof that taking the easy route would never be an option in his life. Watching him, I became determined to work hard and work smart, as well as to gain knowledge I could share with others in an effort to make a true difference in the world.)

To reduce America's debt, our government must either reduce spending, increase taxes, or do a bit of both. And as I've not yet seen significant decreases in national spending, I foresee only one true debt-reducing alternative on the horizon. You know well what that is.

In early 2022, President Joe Biden proposed a budget that called for the implementation of a "billionaires' tax" that was said to affect only the very richest of Americans. Not meaning to sound overly political here, but how many times do you see a tax imposed on one group of people that doesn't eventually work its way down to the rest of us?

Other changes in the tax codes also were being considered, as this book was updated at the end of 2024. There was talk of treating "non-qualified" investment money differently for tax purposes or changing tax-savings strategies such as the "back door" Roth IRA conversion. We'll look at this in more detail later in this chapter.

But let's first begin our look at one of the most basic tax-planning strategies by understanding why such strategies are necessary in the first place.

Required Minimum Distributions: The stranger you will come to know

If tax-deferred retirement savings plans such as the traditional IRA and 401(k) seemed like a good deal to workers, that's probably because they were. People needing every buck they could get to raise young families could make contributions toward their own retirement and have those contributions reduce their tax bill immediately. Furthermore, that invested money had the potential to grow tax-deferred until such time as distributions were taken from the account, presumably in retirement. What's not to like? Sign me up.

There was a tradeoff, of course, one we all knew of even if we didn't think much about it back then. A time would come later in life when we would have to start paying tax on that money. But when you're thirty-five, forty-five, or even fifty-five, you tell yourself that this tax bill is something you'll worry about when that time comes.

Well, now you're suddenly sixty-five—Good Lord, where did the years go?—and "that time" is just ahead on the horizon. You must soon become familiar with required minimum distributions (RMDs), the IRS code that says you must begin taking money from your tax-deferred retirement accounts and paying the tax you've been legally delaying for years. You will take these required withdrawals every year for as long as you still have tax-deferred money, and if you don't "drain the pool" while you are still with us, the tax obligation passes to the inheritors of this money.

Let's explain how an RMD is determined, as not everyone we see is familiar with the process.

Beginning in the year you turn seventy-three (age seventy-five beginning in 2033), you must begin withdrawing money (whether you need to or not) from the pool of tax-deferred assets in your IRA, 401(k), 403(b), TSP, or other "qualified accounts."

The amount in this pool is determined by totaling the value of all your qualified accounts in the year before you must take an RMD. The RMD is determined by dividing that total by a "life expectancy factor" defined by the IRS' Uniform Lifetime Table. This factor, the divisor in the equation, will be lower each year as you get older, meaning the RMD number is likely to increase over time.

The result of all this math is your RMD for the year, and you will pay tax—at your ordinary tax rate—on every penny you are obligated to withdraw. To show how serious the IRS is about finally getting its hands on this money, there is a 25 percent penalty on money that is not withdrawn. This penalty can be reduced to 10 percent if the error is corrected quickly.

This requirement catches too many people by surprise. We had a client who, we realized shortly after meeting him, had not taken his first

RMD. He didn't need the money for income, he didn't know about the rule, and he surely didn't know about the penalty. Fortunately, we worked with an accountant to help him resolve his issues with the IRS. We then set him up to take monthly withdrawals that would meet his annual RMD and worked further on a plan that would allow him to pass on his assets to his grandkids in a tax-efficient manner.

Let's illustrate how RMDs are determined with an example.

John turned seventy-three in 2023. At the end of 2022, the financial agency(s) managing his money reported he had $600,000 in an IRA produced from a rollover of his 401(k). He had another $20,000 in a separate IRA he opened while still contributing to his 401(k). His total pool of qualified money at the end of 2022 was $620,000. For his first RMD in 2023, John divided that total by 27.4, the IRS divisor that took effect after a change in the Uniform Lifetime Table that year.[32] The result, $22,627, was added to John's taxable income for 2023, though he had until April 1, 2024, to take his *first* distribution. All subsequent distributions must be taken by December 31 of each year.

John's wife, Mary, also has an IRA. When she must begin taking RMDs, she will do so based only on the value of her qualified account(s). Money must be taken (and taxed) from her account, and not from that of her husband, and vice versa.

How John goes about taking his RMDs can be a strategic move we can help with.

Many people, you see, don't understand how an RMD can be taken. Do I do it all in a lump sum? Can I take a bit at a time throughout the year as long as I meet my annual number? Can I take everything from just one of my qualified accounts, or do I have to take a bit from each one?

Not meaning to get cute here, but the answer is: Yes, you can do any of the above, with one major exception.

---

[32] Prior to 2022, the IRS Uniform Lifetime Table reflected a lower "life expectancy factor" that effectively increased the amount of an annual RMD. In 2021, for example, the life expectancy factor at age seventy-two was 25.6. Had "John" turned seventy-two in 2021, his RMD on a qualified total of $620,000 would have been $24,218, considerably more than his $22,627 figure after the 2022 change.

The IRS requires that the RMD amount on a 401(k), 403(b), or 457(b) account be taken directly from that account. Here is another reason why we suggest that clients roll over such accounts into a self-controlled IRA shortly after ending their employment through either job change or retirement. You might well have multiple IRA accounts by the time you retire, and the IRS does not require a distribution to be taken from each as long as the total required distribution is met. The IRA rollover itself is not a taxable event, and the taxpayer will have more options in how money in an IRA is invested, as well as how it is withdrawn to meet RMDs.

The challenge is to take distributions in a way that works best for your tax situation.

Here is where working with a tax professional and financial professional can be helpful. Here is where we might look at which of your tax-deferred assets are performing better than others and might be producing profits that are ready for "harvesting." Here is where we might look at taking distributions at market-friendly times instead of waiting to take a lump-sum distribution at year's end. Remember, the IRS cares only that you meet your annual required number and pay the tax on that money. It doesn't care so much about what qualified assets you tap to meet it.

Strategy: Pay your bill when taxes are "on sale"

Again, the most important thing to remember is that this qualified money has been saved (and hopefully grown) untaxed all these years, but it's inevitable that the butcher's bill will come due in time. This brings up the following question: If you must pay this tax bill eventually, why not do it when tax rates are lower?

It almost strains credulity to say it, but taxes are "on sale" (as illustrated by the earlier chart) as this book was being written, and this "sale" is scheduled to continue through the end of 2025. And while I don't pretend to speak for everyone, I feel safe in saying that most people I know would rather buy, let's say, home heating oil, when the average price per gallon in Michigan was lower. It soared to $4.45 on average in March 2022 but dropped to $3.06 on average in September 2024.[33][34] As the age-old saying goes, you can pay me now or pay me later, gambling as you do so that prices are lower now than they will be in the future. And when it comes to taxes, you already know what I believe the future holds.

This is why, when we see people with a high balance in a 401(k) or IRA, we talk about strategic ways to potentially reduce that balance during tax-advantageous times such as the ones still present in 2024 and 2025. This strategy usually involves moving money out of tax-deferred accounts—and paying the inevitable tax at a time when tax rates are known to be lower—before RMDs take effect at a time when future rates are uncertain.

Sometimes we're fortunate to talk to people at an earlier time in life, ideally in their forties or early fifties, about the strategic importance of building up tax-free resources in a Roth IRA or a permanent insurance policy. We might talk, for instance, about the future tax advantages of investing in a Roth 401(k) should your employer offer this option. Or, maybe we can convince older Americans to pass these tax-saving strategies down to their adult children.

Let's look in more detail at a popular strategy for helping to reduce one's pool of soon-to-be-taxed retirement money through the use of the tax-free Roth IRA.

Strategy: Turn tax-deferred money into tax-free assets

We just touched briefly on the strategy of withdrawing tax-deferred money now—before RMDs take effect—and paying the inevitable taxes while rates are lower.

---

[33] U.S. Energy Information Administration. September 25, 2024. "Weekly Michigan No. 2 Heating Oil Residential Price"
https://www.eia.gov/dnav/pet/hist/LeafHandler.ashx?n=PET&s=W_EPD2F_PRS_SMI_DP G&f=W

[34] U.S. Energy Information Administration. September 18, 2024. "Petroleum and Other Liquids: Michigan" https://www.eia.gov/dnav/pet/PET_PRI_WFR_DCUS_SMI_W.htm

Now, what might you do with that money after taking the distribution and paying the tax? The IRS doesn't care. Uncle Sam has gotten his cut, and what remains of the distribution is yours to do with as you please. But before you begin planning a big trip to Venice or Vegas, let's first consider the option to continue growing that money in a tax-free vehicle.

The tax-free Roth IRA

The Roth IRA is such a vehicle. Unlike the traditional IRA, Roth accounts are funded with *after-tax* contributions. These accounts have the potential to grow tax-free, and there is no tax owed when distributions are taken (once certain conditions are met).[35] Roth IRAs also come without RMDs, and they can be passed tax-free to inheritors, something that can't be said of traditional IRAs that might be inherited. Money taken from a Roth account is not part of the income equation that affects either Social Security taxation or the monthly Medicare Part B premium, as defined elsewhere in this chapter.

The popular "Roth conversion strategy" involves moving money out of a traditional IRA or another qualified account, paying the tax on the money taken in the tax year of the withdrawal, then re-investing the remaining balance in the tax-free Roth. It's important to note here that these conversions must be done before RMDs start, as the IRS does not allow RMDs to be converted to Roth accounts.

A few more necessary comments on the Roth IRA before we move into another tax-free vehicle worthy of consideration.

The amount one can contribute annually to a Roth IRA (as well as a traditional IRA) is limited. In 2024, that annual contribution limit was $7,000 for active participants, though people aged fifty and over could

---

[35] Money from a Roth IRA can be withdrawn without tax consequences if taken after age fifty-nine and a half, and if money has been in the account for more than five years. Special circumstances, such as the purchase of a first home, can allow some tax-free withdrawals of the after-tax principal invested in the account. Source: IRS. 2024. "About Publication 509-B, Distributions from Individual Retirement Accounts (IRAs)" https://www.irs.gov/forms-pubs/about-publication-590-b

make an additional $1,000 "catch-up" contribution.[36] Income limits also affect the ability to make a Roth contribution. In 2024, a single tax filer with a modified adjusted gross income (MAGI) of under $161,000 or a couple filing jointly with a MAGI under $240,000 could make Roth contributions.[37] Moreover, a person must be receiving "earned income"—money from wages, tips, commissions, self-employment, etc.—to be eligible to make a Roth contribution.

But while *contributions* to a Roth are limited, *conversions* from a traditional IRA into a Roth are not. As a result, higher earners who are not allowed to make direct contributions to a Roth can still get money into one through what is commonly called the "back door" Roth conversion.

Despite what the name might suggest, this strategy is perfectly legal. It involves making contributions to a traditional IRA—which unlike the Roth has no income limits affecting those who can participate—then converting that money (after paying taxes, of course) into a Roth. To make the best use of the conversion feature, you should ideally have the money to pay the taxes due upon conversion from an outside source and not have it deducted from the converted amount.

As noted above, legislation that would reduce some of the tax benefits available through the back-door Roth passed in the House but was stalled in the Senate, meaning the back-door option remains viable at the time of the writing of this book.

One final note on Roth conversions. The challenge is doing them without having the additional taxable income elevate you into a higher tax bracket. Here is where my team works closely with several local CPAs who can look more closely at your current tax structure and advise on times when conversions might be done most strategically.

We are more inclined, for example, to do gradual conversions over a period of several years. Doing so incurs less taxable income each year

---

[36] IRS. August 20, 2024. "Retirement topics – IRA contribution limits"
https://www.irs.gov/retirement-plans/plan-participant-employee/retirement-topics-ira-contribution-limits
[37] Charles Schwab. 2024. "2023-2024 Roth IRA Contribution Limits"
https://www.schwab.com/ira/roth-ira/contribution-limits

than, let's say, converting a $500,000 IRA in one lump sum with one huge tax bill.

We also look for opportunities to fill up a tax-bracket "bucket" to its brim without overflowing. In other words, how much additional taxable income can a person in the 12 percent tax bracket take on in any one year before overspilling into the 22 percent bracket? How much might be converted this year, and how much might be delayed until following years? And, perhaps more importantly, how might we get these conversions done before 2026 when tax brackets are scheduled to reset to 2017 levels?

Remember, too, that it's also important to complete Roth conversions prior to reaching RMD starting age. RMDs cannot be used to fund a Roth, though any money withdrawn above the RMD number can be converted.

The tax-free advantages of indexed universal insurance

But regardless of what the future holds for the Roth, the tax-advantageous nature of whole-life insurance is likely to remain available.

We sometimes encounter clients who have no immediate need for the qualified money they've been forced to take through RMDs. (Yeah, this happens more often than you might think.) Not needing this money for essential living expenses and having other sources available for the "fun" things they enjoy about retirement, they're looking for ways to make their money continue to work for them.

Here is where we might discuss taking the money they've just paid taxes on and leveraging it into a larger source of future tax-free cash that will eventually become available to someone of their choosing.

We talked earlier about how whole-life policies such as the Indexed Universal Life offer the potential for growth as well as a tax-free death benefit to beneficiaries. They also can be a source of tax-free income and possible long-term care funding for the insured. But we also must mention the IUL's potential role in helping convert your pool of tax-deferred money into future tax-free assets.

The idea is similar to the Roth conversion, except that instead of putting RMD funds into the Roth, a person might consider using them to pay the premiums on an IUL policy. By using some (or all) of these new-found funds to pay a yearly IUL premium of, say, $20,000, a person over the course of fewer than seven years could have a fully funded $140,000 policy that could produce a tax-free death benefit of anywhere from $300,000 to $500,000 depending on your age, health and the policy you select. Don't forget, either, the potential for tax-free income for the insured (via loans taken against the death benefit), or the prospect of purchasing long-term care benefits that such policies can offer.

Ideally, we encourage people to make investments in tax-free vehicles at a younger age. The purchase of whole life insurance is one such option.

People with still-young families might consider the cash value feature of indexed universal life policies. Not only does the IUL offer the traditional financial protection for loved ones through a tax-free death benefit, but it also has the potential for growth in cash value through credited interest tied to an underlying market index to which the policy is linked. The cash value could be used to pay future premiums as long as the credited interest is sufficient and the policy has enough cash value to keep the policy in force. It also can provide a source of tax-free income via loans taken against the cash value.

This choice of insurance options can be especially challenging for young families.

Many, for instance, rely initially on life insurance provided by an employer. This coverage is often term insurance, which means that when a worker leaves that employer (or retires), they typically must secure new coverage or go without it. This coverage can become more expensive as one gets older, which is why we encourage our clients to obtain their own life insurance coverage at a relatively young age.

Other people might consider the option of paid-up insurance as a protection and tax strategy. One might, for instance, take a one-time withdrawal from an IRA and use the after-tax remainder as a single-pay premium on an IUL. Or, one might use a series of IRA withdrawals-as a 5-to-7 pay premium that can ultimately produce a paid-up policy that can provide future tax-free income (via loans taken against the cash value of the policy) as well as a tax-free death benefit for surviving loved ones.

A younger worker might also consider the Roth 401(k) option offered by many employers. Unlike the traditional 401(k), your contributions here are made on an after-tax basis, meaning you don't get an immediate tax break. But you'll get your money tax-free when taking qualified distributions in retirement when needed, as Roth funds are not subject to RMDs.

OK, I can hear you saying, "What? I'm losing my tax break today? Why should I give that up when I need every cent I can get with two teenagers suddenly making our current house seem very cramped? Worse yet, they're both talking about wanting their own cars, and one wants to go to law school."

I know, it's a tough tradeoff. But that's when we can show you reports that break down the difference between what you're saving today when investing in a tax-deferred 401(k) versus what you might save in future taxes by instead investing after-tax money into a Roth IRA or purchasing a whole-life insurance policy.

This is what real tax-planning is all about.

Other "hidden" taxes in retirement

There are several other taxes that are unique to retirement, as well as some surcharges and takebacks that, while not technically taxes, have the effect of reducing how much of your retirement money you get to keep.

Let's first consider the taxation of Social Security benefits. This is a prospect that surprises many seniors who remember having a Social Security tax—7.65 percent—withheld from their regular paychecks as a means of funding both Social Security and Medicare. The thought of now possibly having to pay another tax on benefits received produces a sour taste in the mouths of many people.

It's worth noting here that not everyone will owe this tax. In fact, when Social Security was first implemented in 1935 as a part of President Franklin Roosevelt's "New Deal" recovery from The Great Depression, FDR promised that Americans who suddenly were being taxed to fund a new program would never pay tax once they started receiving its benefits. By 1983, however, concern over the long-term viability of the program prompted President Ronald Reagan to sign legislation imposing a tax on up to 50 percent of benefits received by people whose "provisional income" exceeded a certain level.[38] Just a decade later, President Bill Clinton signed into law an increase on that taxation, one that could tax up to 85 percent of benefits for people with higher levels of income, as reflected in the below chart.

Social Security Taxation

Filing status	Provisional income	Benefits subject to taxation
Single	Less than $25,000	No benefits taxable
Single	>$25,000 and <$34,000	Up to 50% of benefits taxable
Single	More than $34,000	Up to 85% of benefits taxable
Married filing jointly	Less than $32,000	No benefits taxable
Married filing jointly	>$32,000 and <$44,000	Up to 50% of benefits taxable
Married filing jointly	More than $44,000	Up to 85% of benefits taxable

---

[38] Provisional income, also known as "combined income" by the Social Security Administration, is defined as adjusted gross income plus non-taxable interest plus one-half of all Social Security benefits. Source: Julia Kagan. Investopedia. October 8, 2022. "Provisional Taxes: What They are and how They Work"
https://www.investopedia.com/terms/p/provisional-income.asp

As you can see, the income levels that prompt Social Security taxation aren't especially high by today's standards. These were actually considered a "tax on the rich" when they were implemented in 1983 and expanded in 1994, but they've never been adjusted for inflation since. Consequently, many readers of this book might well be paying tax on their monthly benefits.

Here is another reason why we emphasize tax-planning strategies. We will work with you to find ways to help keep your provisional income—which *does not* include distributions taken from tax-free vehicles such as the Roth IRA—below the levels that precipitate taxation where possible. The difference between paying taxes on Social Security benefits and not doing so could amount to as much as tens of thousands of dollars over a normal retirement period.

While on the subject of Social Security, let's also look here at the "earnings test" applied to people who continue to receive wages while taking benefits before reaching full retirement age (FRA).

The Social Security Administration doesn't forbid "early retirees" from continuing to work, but it does impose some limits. In 2024, people taking benefits before FRA could earn up to $22,320 in wages without consequence. For earnings above that limit, however, the SSA will take back $1 in benefits for every $2 earned above the limit. The money is withheld in the form of reduced benefit checks.[39]

Example: John "retired" at age sixty-two and began receiving benefits. But he continued to work part-time—in part because he enjoyed it and, frankly, he needed the income—and earned $28,320 that year (a figure I chose only because it rounds up conveniently from the earnings limit). John made $6,000 over the limit, which means that in the following year, the SSA will withhold $3,000 in benefits by reducing his monthly check until that number is reached.

Now for some better news should you postpone retirement until FRA. You can earn up to $59,520 without incurring a "takeback" in the

---

[39] Tim Parker. Investopedia. September 24, 2024. "How Much Can I Make on Social Security?" https://www.investopedia.com/articles/personal-finance/120715/how-does-my-parttime-job-affect-social-security.asp

months of the calendar year before you reach FRA, and the takeback then is only $1 for every $3 over the limit. Better yet, you can earn as much as you can without incurring a takeback after reaching FRA. Moreover, the benefits withheld before then will gradually be paid back (through higher benefit checks) at that time.[40]

I mention this "takeback" primarily because I see clients who believe they can retire "early" and live comfortably on a reduced Social Security check when coupled with employment income. They just need to know there is a catch in the plan that can reduce the size of their benefit check.

Finally, let's look at the surcharge that can be applied to the monthly Medicare Part B premium paid by Americans whose modified adjusted gross income (MAGI) exceeds certain thresholds.

As noted in our health care chapter, most Americans will pay a monthly premium of $174.70 for Medicare Part B in 2024.[41] The Medicare Trustees report projects this number could rise to as much as $230 per person in 2029.[42]

But higher earners could have to pay that much or more now. The chart below shows the threshold for higher premiums, which begins for single filers with MAGIs exceeding $103,000 and couples filing jointly at $206,000 in 2022. This premium surcharge, which is based on the MAGI of two years preceding the tax year in question, has five step-ups.[43]

Clearly, working with tax-savvy professionals, such as the members of my team alongside your CPA or tax advisor, can help develop ways to keep your *taxable* income below points that incur higher taxes or surcharges, even as we work to keep your after-tax income at a level with which you are comfortable.

---

[40] Ibid.
[41] Centers for Medicare & Medicaid Services. October 11, 2023. "2024 Medicare Parts A & B Premiums and Deductibles"
https://www.rrb.gov/Newsroom/NewsReleases/MedicarePartBPremium#
[42] Virginia Pelley. Forbes. September 3, 2024. "Medicare Part B: Coverage, Costs And Eligibility" https://www.forbes.com/health/medicare/medicare-part-b/
[43] Medicare.gov. 2024. "2024 Medicare costs" https://www.medicare.gov/publications/11579-medicare-costs.pdf

If your yearly income in 2022 was:[44]			You pay each month (in 2024)
File individual tax return	File joint tax return	File married & separate tax return	
$103,000 or less	$206,000 or less	$103,000 or less	Your plan premium
Above $103,000 up to $129,000	Above $206,000 up to $258,000	Not applicable	$12.90 + your plan premium
Above $129,000 up to $161,000	Above $258,000 up to $322,000	Not applicable	$33.30 + your plan premium
Above $161,000 up to $193,000	Above $322,000 up to $386,000	Not applicable	$53.80 + your plan premium
Above $193,000 and less than $500,000	Above $386,000 and less than $750,000	Above $103,000 and less than $397,000	$74.20 + your plan premium
$500,000 or above	$750,000 and above	$397,000 and above	$81.00 + your plan premium

And now that we've talked about keeping as much of your retirement money as possible via reduced taxes, let's look at ways of continuing to grow your money in the years just before and following retirement. For that discussion, I'll turn things over to my husband, Nolan McIntosh, the wealth strategist/risk management professional in our family and in our firm.

---

[44] Ibid.

CHAPTER 6

Strategies: Why Take the Risk?

By Nolan McIntosh
Investment Adviser Representative, McIntosh and Associates

When it comes to managing investment risk, especially for our retirement-age clients, I often take a cue from Warren Buffett, long acknowledged as one of America's smartest investors. For it was the Oracle of Omaha who once said, using words to this effect: If you absolutely don't need to assume more risk, why do it?

It's a message we share often with our McIntosh and Associates clients, many of whom are preparing for or actually in retirement.

Now, please don't misunderstand me. I'm not opposed to the idea of risk. It has its place in all phases of our investment lives, especially in our younger years. But our capacity for risk changes—for most people—as we get older.

Think back for a moment to when we first started investing in our future. We typically did so by putting a bit of each paycheck into an employer-sponsored 401(k) or other defined contribution retirement savings program. We got an immediate tax break by doing so, and we usually took on a higher degree of risk in choosing how that money was invested.

And why not? "No risk, no reward" was a concept we readily accepted whether we were putting money on Apple stock or, let's say, the Detroit Tigers in the World Series. Sometimes you win (on both Apple and the Tigers in 1984) and sometimes you lose (the Tigers in 2012. In four straight to San Francisco? Seriously?). But such is the game of life.

In our younger years, we could take more chances when growing our assets, knowing we had time to ride out the occasional, inevitable downturns in the market, painful though they were. Many of our clients today still remember the "Black Monday" crash of 1987, a 22 percent drop in the Dow in a single day. Others have more recent bad memories of the "dot-com bubble burst" of 2001 and the "Great Recession" of late 2007 through early 2009.

But they also remember the go-go days of the 1990s as well as an unprecedented bull market from 2009 through 2019. Even during the darkest of market days, we assured ourselves that, in time, our "paper losses" would recover and continue to grow if only we "held the line" and waited for the market to do what it normally does. And more times than not, that patience paid off in portfolio growth.

But the years just before and actually into retirement are different times, and suddenly it's necessary to take a new look at the risk we take with our retirement savings.

Now time is no longer on our side. Now any sustained market-related loss in portfolio value is more than just a "paper loss." Now we're looking at an actual decrease in cash you will likely need—and possibly soon—for retirement income. Now is a time to consider taking more of a defensive approach to your retirement nest egg, one that seeks continued growth but likely at a more conservative, less risky pace.

To quote Mr. Buffett again, "Changes in latitude require changes in attitude."

(Sorry, wrong Buffett. But Jimmy's famous song makes the same point.)

As *Warren* Buffett might ask: Why, as a retirement-age investor, would you take the risk necessary to get a 15 percent gain in your portfolio when all you need for growth is a 5 percent gain that beats the rate of inflation? To add some timeliness to that comment, inflation in 2024 has slowed to 2.5 percent in August 2024, but as we all know, that rate is subject to change based on a variety of factors, making it important to continually update your plan.[45] However, Buffett's main point remains the same.

The race isn't over

By now, you may be asking yourself, "Why do I want to take *any* risk with my retirement savings? I spent forty years in the daily rat race, working hard for the money needed to raise a family, make ends meet, and put away whatever I could toward my retirement. Why can't I just enjoy living on that money now instead of worrying about continuing to grow it?"

Fair point. I understand the sentiment, really.

Some people can do exactly that. They've earned and saved and invested well enough to assure themselves the reliable income necessary, both in the near and long term, for the retirement lifestyle of their choice without having to worry about creating additional wealth. Bravo for them.

But most people aren't that blessed. Even those who've assured themselves a steady stream of sustainable income for today have some concerns about meeting the rising expenses of tomorrow. Taxes will probably rise. Medical expenses are likely to increase. Costly long-term nursing care may become necessary. Inflation will continue to be a factor. Will you have the means to pay for all those rising costs?

These are all valid concerns that highlight the need for continued growth in your retirement savings, even as you begin to tap those savings as part of providing your own paycheck.

I know, it doesn't seem fair. You spent years running hard in an attempt to grow wealth, and now you learn you may still have a few more laps to run.

Well, there is some good news. For while the race may not yet be over, you don't necessarily have to run at the same pace you once did. Putting our racing metaphor aside, what we're talking about here is

---

[45] Trading Economics. 2024. "United States Inflation Rate" https://tradingeconomics.com/united-states/inflation-cpi

developing a new approach to the level of investment risk you now are willing to take to make your money grow.

Retirement age, in my opinion, is a time when protecting your assets takes precedence over assuming extra risk in order to grow them. It's sometimes said that, in retirement, a loss hurts more than a gain feels good. This is why as a wealth manager working with retirement-age clients, I often hedge more against loss than concentrate mainly on building wealth—the main goal of many in the financial services industry. To be sure, we also work to grow wealth, but we've also found that people of retirement age are more comfortable with avoiding losses than they are in growing wealth.

Or, as more than one client has told us, "At this stage in our lives, we're more comfortable with money in the bank as opposed to money in the market."

This is part of the transition that comes as retirement approaches. A shift needs to happen, and that's hard for some. People spent years accumulating assets, and many have done a good job of it. But now they need a shift in mindset, one that may involve protecting assets more than growing them. It's sometimes hard to see this through a different lens.

This is especially true when they hear a friend, co-worker, or family member bragging about making, say, a 16 percent return on an investment. They listen to this kind of boast, true or not, and immediately think, "Hey, I'd like to get that, too."

What they're not thinking about, however, is how that friend's financial situation is likely very different from their own.

Maybe that neighbor is in a better place emotionally or financially to take more risk in the hope of realizing a greater reward. Maybe that family member isn't facing the immediate medical or financial concerns that you are. Maybe that co-worker isn't relying on their investments for income. (And believe me, your perspective will change when you're relying on your investments for income.)

You suddenly can't afford to take the chances you once did. You now find yourself wanting more principal protection than asset growth. To quote Warren Buffett once more: Why take the risk in reaching for a 16 percent return when you need considerably less to keep pace with inflation and still grow your retirement savings portfolio?

Admittedly, not everyone shares this philosophy. Some retirees are very comfortable staying in "the investment game" they've played most of their life. They already have the dependable income they need without tapping their investments, and they consequently can take more risk with those investments. Some actually enjoy the challenge of continuing to "play the market."

But again, most people we see are not in that (river)boat. They also are looking for growth but are willing to take only low or moderate risk to attain it, albeit at a lower level of return. Some can accept no risk at all. Everyone's situation is different, and the challenge for my team is to address every unique situation.

There are investment tools available for all different levels of risk tolerance. But before we decide which tool to use in your special situation, we first need to know more about what we're setting out to do, and what kind of risk level you are willing to take to get there.

Let's look at how we go about doing that.

Determine your risk level

As my wife Mindy mentioned in Chapter 1, one of the first things we set out to determine in the FOCUS part of our FOCUS Wealth Plan is the level of risk you are comfortable taking with your investments. She talked in Chapter 2 about how part of our Analysis process examines how much risk is actually present in your current portfolio.

Now as part of our investment process, we'll explore how we might structure an investment portfolio, or make adjustments to your existing one, that balances the need for continued growth with the risk tolerance you are comfortable with, a level you've helped us determine. More on developing such a portfolio is coming in the next section of this chapter, as is a discussion of modifying that portfolio as conditions change.

But let's first look at how we determine your current level of risk tolerance, one that may be very different at age sixty-two than it was at thirty-two.

Using an interview process included in a computer software program (Riskalyze), an individual (or both spouses in a couple) is assigned a risk tolerance number from 1 to 100. Lower numbers indicate a low acceptance of risk, while people with higher numbers tend to be more aggressive.

But we also ask many other questions as well, ones not covered in standard software, in an attempt to further understand your goals and how we can best help you achieve them without bringing added stress into your life.

We need to know, for example, your goals for the portion of the retirement assets in the wealth management part of your portfolio. Are you looking for continued wealth accumulation? Additional income? Or, most likely, a combination of both? We ask about the time frame of your investment strategy; how long are you willing to expose these assets to some level of market risk? We'll ask about what percentages you would like to win, and what you could tolerate losing. We do this to find out what kind of reward is being sought, because we all know that more risk is involved when trying to achieve a greater reward.

The risk analysis results we develop surprise some people, many of whom learn they are not the riverboat gamblers they imagined themselves to be. For example:

It's not uncommon to hear a client say, "I could probably drop 10 percent without losing any sleep." Well, that's fine and good—until they actually lose 10 percent of their portfolio. Or, when you remind them that a 10 percent decline in the $500,000 balance of their 401(k) is $50,000. You can often sense their confidence beginning to wane a bit shortly after putting the percentage of a loss into actual dollars.

I think it was boxer Mike Tyson who once said, "Everyone has a plan until they get punched in the mouth." That's the way it is with many people who take a hit to their investment portfolio, especially at retirement age. That hit hurts even more when you realize you don't make up a 10 percent loss with just a 10 percent gain, but that it takes more like a 12 percent gain to get back what you've lost.

(Really, just do the math. A 10 percent loss of a $500,000 account balance is $50,000, leaving you with $450,000. To get back to "even" requires a $50,000 gain that now represents an almost 12 percent growth of your $450,000 balance.)

Another part of the Riskalyze program takes an in-depth look at the risk level of your current investments. Many people who purchased investment products described as having only conservative or moderate risk levels are often surprised to learn that these investments now have a higher risk exposure than they initially believed, often because of changing conditions over the years since they made the investment.

This really isn't all that surprising. Let's face it, not everyone knows the level of risk they're actually taking in their retirement investments. They've likely followed a buy-and-hold pattern with their 401(k) investments over all their working years, and they've rarely (if ever) changed anything. The risk level they had when they started the plan in their twenties may be the same as they have now in their sixties. Yet when we sit down and show them the level of risk they're taking in their retirement portfolio, they'll often say, "I had no idea. I just kind of let things ride because it had done well for me all these years."

Look, I understand that, I truly do. It's an approach that likely served you well in your working years, your time of "dollar cost averaging" when regular payroll contributions purchased additional shares of an investment as share prices became lower during market downturns. In retirement, however, you are no longer making payroll contributions and aren't likely to be buying additional investment shares. And now it may be time to take another look at things.

Our goal in risk management is to limit the potential for losses, which is especially important for people on the conservative side of the investment spectrum as well as those of retirement age. People willing to accept a little less reward in exchange for taking less risk might be thankful when a Tyson-like punch like the Great Recession—which produced a 35 percent drop in the S&P 500—misses instead of landing flush on the jaw.

A big part of our FOCUS Wealth Plan involves putting some risk mitigation curbs into the plan. The goal is to provide principal protection, income and some liquidity while still keeping other funds active in the market. These market investments can potentially provide a hedge against inflation, the increasing cost of taxes and health care as well as providing funding for possible long-term nursing care in the future. We think it's important to have both stable income and some level of growth-seeking assets in a retirement portfolio. The way we might balance that depends on each individual or couple and finding the balance that's right for each is what makes the process challenging.

The idea is to create risk spectrums that allow people to not be emotionally concerned about what tomorrow might bring, but rather puts them more at ease and in more control when they know their risk level is something they can live with.

Structuring/Adjusting the portfolio

Mindy and I both believe that any retirement plan should include what we call the "3C" components: comfort, confidence, and control. These elements also should be part of the investment side of any plan.

Comfort and confidence, we believe, come initially from completing the first and most important part of our Strategies process. I'm talking here about income planning. Simply put, we believe that people with an established income plan—one that assures a stream of stable, sustainable income for the remainder of their lives—put themselves in a position to make better decisions about the growth of their investment assets.

Control comes from knowing you can make adjustments to both your overall retirement plan and investment plan as conditions change—health conditions, family situations, inflation, and market performance. You need to know that you and the financial professional you are working with can make any adjustments necessary when changing conditions dictate.

Let's look at all of that a bit more closely, beginning with the importance of having "stable" income.

Stable income—what was once called "mailbox income"—comes from dependable regular sources such as Social Security, annuity payments, a pension (if you have one), dividends and interest, and maybe even rental income. But it's not uncommon for people to turn to their retirement savings for additional income to supplement what "fixed" sources fail to provide. Filling this "income gap" is a pretty normal part of any retirement plan.

The trouble, however, comes when people rely too heavily on at-risk market investments to supplement their fixed income. People in this situation can face a double whammy when taking income from assets that could be losing value because of inevitable market downturns. Eventually, they begin to dip into their invested principal, and now the prospect of running out of money in retirement suddenly becomes very real.

I've always believed that investments should be used for our "wants" as opposed to our "needs." Let me explain that. We may not absolutely need a new car, but we may want one. Or, we want to go on a dream vacation to Europe, but we don't absolutely need to. You may want to pass money on to your kids, but you may not absolutely need to.

This is where we need to separate things. Your needs are the necessities of daily living—food, clothing, utilities, housing costs and repairs, and transportation. Your needs should ideally be paid for from your stable income side.

Your wants, on the other hand, should come from your investment side. But it's only after we establish your income side to meet all of your needs that we can open up a window and take some risk (at whatever level you are comfortable) on the investment side.

Now when you decide that you either want or need a new car, you can decide whether the time is right to take money from your investment portfolio, or from what assets we might tap. Or, if you want to take that European vacation, you might be a bit more aggressive in how you save for that trip when knowing that your income needs are met.

Our goal in setting up the investment side of your retirement plan is to provide a combination of protection (as determined by a client's risk tolerance) and growth. How we work to achieve this balance using a mix of stocks, bonds, cash, and other potential investment and insurance products varies greatly from client to client.

As noted earlier, many retirement-age people we see tend to be more conservative in their approach to investing. Not a thing in the world wrong with that. There are problems, however, with being too cautious, just as there are in being overly ambitious.

For while there is comfort in having cash during retirement, there also is often little to no growth in it. Interest rates on bank deposits and CDs fell to a mere pittance in the low-interest rate climate borne of the Great Recession. Growth in safe and secure bank accounts didn't keep pace with inflation in the years of 2 percent annual hikes in the Consumer Price Index, much less amid the 7 and 8 percent rises of 2022. And while there is certainly a need for some cash (generally for emergency purposes) in any retirement plan, it's also true that depending heavily on cash as an investment is a way of, as the expression goes, losing money safely. As mentioned, in 2024, the interest rate has consistently been trending down. However, we also know how quickly things can change, so it's good to constantly update your plans accordingly.

Bonds tend to produce a slightly higher rate of interest than do bank deposits, but even they are no longer the reliable refuge they once were when stock prices were depressed. Still, bonds can hold a place in the portfolio of investors seeking income and some measure of protection. Let's briefly look at why that is.

Bonds pay a fixed rate of interest for as long as you hold them. Their protection comes in a promise from the bond issuer to return an investor's principal in full when the bond reaches maturity. But nothing is guaranteed, making bonds different from bank deposits that are protected (for up to $250,000 per account title) by the FDIC. A bond issuer could go out of business and default on the bond, which makes the promises to repay the principal worthless. Moreover, bonds traded before reaching maturity are subject to price and interest fluctuation risk.

Example: In times of rising interest rates, the bond you own that pays 3 percent interest will not be as attractive to a potential buyer as a new bond issued at a 3.25 percent rate. You probably won't get back what you initially invested if you sell your bond. Should interest rates decline, however, your 3 percent bond might look good to a buyer who can get only 2.75 percent interest on a new bond. Such a buyer might pay a premium to buy your higher-paying bond.

Stocks, mutual funds, and ETFs are what they are, rising and falling in value on a day-to-day basis. Investing in stocks comes with no degree of security, but there is potential for income (especially when investing in dividend-producing stock) as well as growth. It also should go without saying that there also is the potential for loss of invested principal. Your portfolio's level of exposure to individual stocks or funds should be determined largely by your tolerance of risk.

There is one financial tool that we often recommend, however, that comes with a level of protection as well as the potential to produce income and growth. It's an insurance product Mindy and I believe has at least a place in the retirement and investment plans of many of our clients as appropriate.

I'm talking again about the fixed index annuity (FIA), which Mindy described in an earlier chapter. The FIA, in short, is an insurance contract that promises regular annuity payments (often for the life of the annuitant if the contract is so structured) in exchange for the premium paid. The guarantee to make payments is supported by the claims-paying ability of the insurance company that issues the contract, and these companies are regulated by the states in which they operate.

The beauty of the FIA, in my view, is its ability to generate interest based on the growth of an external market index, subject to cap or other limit set by the company, with a guarantee against loss of principal due to market performance. Let's say that again. Growth of the annuity is created by *credited interest* based on the performance of an external market index (Dow Jones Industrial Average, S&P 500, NASDAQ, etc.) that the annuity holder elects. The issuing insurance calculates the annuity owner's potential interest, usually annually, based on the index's performance.

Example: If the DJIA goes up 12 percent over the contract year, the annuitant (you) will receive a capped portion of that gain—let's say, 6 percent in this example—in interest credited to your account value. If the market rises only 3 percent, you get 3 percent. But if the market falls 5 percent, you lose nothing in the account value that is reset annually to reflect previous interest credits. Keep in mind that if you purchase optional annuity riders, these fees will still be deducted even in years where you earn no interest. And as with all financial vehicles, the FIA involves terms and conditions, fees and potential surrender penalties for early withdrawals.

Yeah, I know. Annuities are a dirty word to some people, especially given potential fees and market volatility associated with the variable annuity that was the flavor of the day during the go-go days of the 1990s. But it's my view that the principal-protected FIA deserves a look and may have a place in the retirement plan of someone looking for elements of protection, income, and potential growth in their investment strategy.

To repeat a central point of this chapter, the level of risk you decide to take in your investment portfolio is entirely up to you. Our job is to help you build such a portfolio, or revise your current one, to meet whatever level you are comfortable with.

And, frankly, we sometimes meet clients who have not done an especially good job of saving, investing, and growing their retirement money. These folks may have to take a bit more risk, even later in life, to get where they want or need to be. Some need their retirement savings for essential income, and sadly, if they don't do more to grow what they have, they stand a chance of running out of money. I work with them to help improve their position without employing a Vegas-style "play it all on red" approach.

I also stand ready to help you make adjustments to your investment plan during sustained market downturns or times when you need additional income from your retirement savings.

Look, we all know it's normal for markets to go up and down. We also know that we're not going to win at everything we try. But at McIntosh and Associates, we also believe that when our FOCUS Wealth Plan is deployed, people can be in a better position to "shelter in place" when a market storm is upon us. This "shelter" is provided when you are receiving reliable income that meets your routine expenses every month—as well as helping provide for some of the "fun" things of retirement—that is not completely exposed to the winds of market volatility. The rush to make emotional investment decisions—often many of them bad ones—during a market downturn can be reduced or even eliminated.

I'm pleased to report that we didn't get a lot of calls from clients during times like March of 2020 when the market dropped—briefly, thank goodness—more than 30 percent in the first days of the COVID-19 pandemic. (Market indexes rebounded to record highs just months later.) That's not to suggest, however, that we won't be active and contact a client if we feel that adjustments are necessary, or if they become nervous about their income or investment plan.

Unlike some advisors who like to call clients only when times are good and say, "Hey, look what we did," but then go mute when times are bad, we want our friends to be looking at their regular statements and telling us about any concerns they have. At any time if someone says, "I just don't like what I'm seeing in the market (or the economy, or events happening elsewhere in the world)," we can make adjustments very rapidly to address their concerns.

Bottom line, anyone can grow assets when market times are good, and I'm not saying I'm any better than any person down the street.

But a true retirement plan involves more than just investing. What makes things most interesting for Mindy and me is putting together all the pieces of the retirement puzzle to produce a clear look at your retirement future. This picture should include reliable income for today and tomorrow, as well as the potential to grow other assets—at a risk level with which you are comfortable—for future needs or wants.

CHAPTER 7

Strategies: Fill in the Family Circle

Much of the previous parts of this book was spent on matters of finance and economics. What might you expect to pay in retirement for this, how much might you need for that, etc. Such discussions about securing income and managing money clearly have an important place in any retirement plan.

But now it's time to consider what some might call a matter of the heart. That is, what happens to those we love after we leave them?

It's not an easy subject for many people to think about, involving as it does our own inevitable demise. But because death is a fact of life that we all must face eventually, it's important in any holistic retirement plan to consider how we might help loved ones when we are no longer able to do so, either because of our passing or mental/physical incapacity.

The fifth Solution piece of our FOCUS Wealth Plan is commonly called "estate" or "legacy" planning by many advisors. But we take a slightly different approach at McIntosh and Associates. We refer to the plans we make for surviving loved ones as our "family circle" planning, a name that reflects how preparations made today can support people who are important to us both before and after our passing. Included later in this chapter, for instance, will be a discussion of funding long-term nursing care, something many clients consider a "burden" they do not want family members to carry. We'll also talk about living wills and powers of attorney—people assigned to make decisions for us when we can no longer make them for ourselves.

We sometimes refer to this part of our planning process as "completing the circle." To not do such planning is, in my view, like trying to complete a puzzle with several pieces missing. Oh, it can be done, I suppose; you'll get a general view of what the picture is supposed to look like. But the puzzle will always be incomplete.

The same thing applies to comprehensive retirement planning. It's just not effective to do all this work in setting up your retirement if you don't also make plans for any assets you might leave behind, especially when they might make life a little easier for the people you love. We often encounter people who understand the importance of doing this, but without professional guidance, they don't know how to go about doing these things.

We actually begin working on this process in our first meeting when we try to establish what's important to a new client. Where does family fit into their retirement goals, both now and in the future? What are their concerns for a surviving spouse? Are they wanting to pass money to heirs? Are they worried about providing for their own care should they need nursing care in the future?

Different people, of course, have different views on the money they take into retirement, to say nothing of what they might leave behind.

Some folks say, with good reason, that they've worked hard for every cent they have, and they intend to spend whatever they have on themselves. OK, I get that. I've actually heard people joke (I hope) about wanting to bounce their last check to a cruise line. Cute, but not a "final planning" approach I would recommend.

Other people are more concerned about leaving money for loved ones. We are here to help them develop plans that can do exactly that and do so in a tax-efficient way. More on that later in this chapter.

But whatever your approach is to money you will no longer be here to use, it's important that we at least talk about a subject many people aren't especially eager to talk about. We're not doing a very good job in developing a financial plan if we don't help people close the loop.

The basics of legacy planning

One of the simplest elements of legacy planning involves some financial housekeeping—the proverbial "getting your affairs in order."

We actually help begin this process during the FOCUS phase of our planning when we work with you to assemble many of the documents—retirement account statements, investment statements, bank accounts, annuity contracts, and insurance policies—that we use in setting up your income plan. To that collection, we'll later add home and property titles, car registrations, and other legal documents you've likely overlooked. The goal is to assemble in one place the important documents you don't want people scrambling to look for when they need to find them and you aren't here to provide directions.

We also urge people to do essential things like updating the beneficiary designations on insurance policies and annuities. We will encourage inclusion of pay-on-death (POD) designations on bank accounts, and transfer-on-death (TOD) assignments on property. These changes, which can be done easily at your bank or county courthouse, can be especially important considering how relationships change over time through disputes, divorce, and, sadly, premature death.

Then, in more cases than not, we help people secure the legal assistance they might require.

A will is a bare minimum

Let me start by saying that I am not an attorney. But I believe that, at the very least, our clients should have a will—one prepared by an estate attorney as opposed to readily available computer software.

Not everyone agrees. Some will argue that people with "simple" assets can prepare their own will and disburse their assets without legal assistance. Unmarried renters, they might say, who have simple bank accounts along with some household possessions and maybe a car can pass their assets to those of their choosing through POD and TOD assignments, as well as proper beneficiary designations on insurance contracts.

I, however, would respectfully suggest that most clients we see, as well as most readers of this book, have assets that are more complex and require more than do-it-yourself remedies.

To not have at least a will that states your intention for the disposition of your assets is inviting trouble. Dying without a will is called dying "*intestate*," and that means a probate court will decide how your earthly possessions are distributed. Probate proceedings are public hearings that can be long and costly, with the court expenses being taken from the value of the estate. Probate decisions may reflect the best judgment of the court, but not necessarily the intentions of the deceased.

Note, too, that even a will must be approved by the probate court, which will decide whether the will's executor has satisfied all debts and taxes owed by the estate before being cleared to distribute assets in accordance with the instructions of the deceased.

Putting more faith in a trust

I'm a bigger believer that most people we see should have a living trust.

This is especially true for clients who have assets over a certain amount, or property or a business interest, or are looking to do something in a strategic way for grandchildren or minor children. Moreover, if a person wants one survivor to inherit more than another and has specific instructions to that effect, we are inclined to suggest a trust no matter how much they have in assets.

Now, not everyone needs a trust, which is slightly more costly to establish than a regular will. For people with less complicated intentions, those who say, "When I pass, my spouse and children will inherit everything,' things may be more cut and dried. Even then, we might encourage this person to see an estate attorney we work closely with to determine how best to protect their wishes.

Still, I would say that some two-thirds of the clients we work with have a trust.

A properly structured and "funded" trust (more on this soon) has several advantages over a will, in my opinion. A trust is not a public-record document and is not subject to approval in probate court. (Though a trust, like a will, can be challenged in a regular court proceeding.) The disposition of assets within a trust is generally done more quickly under the supervision of one or more designated trustee(s). The original "grantor(s)" of the trust can also be its original trustee(s) and retain full control of all its assets until the passing of the original trustee, or both members of a couple. Control of the trust then passes to the designated "successor trustee(s)."

A couple of important legal documents also are included in a typical trust, another strong point in their favor.

One such document is a "living will"—instructions for life-saving medical procedures that may or might not be administered. Also included are power of attorney (POA) designations—two separate documents that assign powers to make a) financial decisions, and b) medical decisions should the grantor become physically or mentally unable to make decisions for themselves. Note that POA designations end at the time of the grantor's death.

It's my strong opinion here that people not participating in a trust at least seek legal advice in setting up POA designations.

We also work with clients and their estate attorneys to properly "fund" assets to a trust. Let's explain that.

A trust is a series of legal documents, part of which establish something akin to a safe. Assets that are properly "titled" to the trust are protected within the safe. Assets not titled to the trust might as well be lying on the floor outside the safe. We often see clients who believe they have a trust that will provide a smooth transition of assets to their heirs. But these heirs sometimes discover only later—sometimes too late—that their benefactors failed to title their holdings within the trust, thus making it as effective as, well, an empty safe.

Inherited IRA and the end of Stretch IRA

Another goal of our Family Circle is to make the passing of legacy gifts not only as simple, but also as tax-friendly as possible.

That can be a challenge when much of an inheritance is received from the untapped balance of an IRA, a 401(k), or other tax-deferred "qualified" account. As you remember from our tax chapter, the IRS is anxious to get its cut of this money that has yet to be taxed. If it doesn't get that cut from you while you are still with us, it will take it from whoever inherits your untaxed balance.

In short, an inherited IRA or other qualified account comes with a tax bill. What you see on the bottom line of your late father's IRA isn't necessarily what you will receive as money in the bank.

There once was a way to reduce the tax obligation on this inherited money. It was such a sweet deal that Congress did away with it.

Until a few years ago, the "stretch IRA" allowed an inheritor to take required minimum distributions based on their age as opposed to that of the deceased account owner. That allowed inheritors to take money in lower amounts and pay less in taxes than did their considerably older benefactor. Inheriting children, and particularly grandchildren, could effectively extend the life of an inherited IRA by stretching out distributions (and the corresponding taxes owed) over the course of their own lifetimes, thus giving the account additional time to grow even as distributions were being taken.

But you know what they say about how nothing good lasts forever.

The SECURE Act of 2019, which took effect January 1, 2020, eliminated the Stretch IRA for most non-spousal beneficiaries. In its place, people inheriting the untaxed balance of an IRA now have only ten years to liquidate the account and, of course, pay the corresponding taxes as they do so. An inheritor can take the money in one lump sum, incurring a big tax bill in the process, or spread distributions out over the ten-year period, taking them at opportune times to do so.

This change has made a big difference in how people approach some retirement plan assets that are handed down to future generations, especially when it comes to second-generation inheritance to grandchildren.

The challenge now is to help inheritors take this money in the most efficient manner possible, as well as to help reinvest that money when future growth is a goal.

Efficiency involves taking taxable distributions at strategic times. Market performance is a factor in this decision, but so are taxes. A person on the lower end of a tax bracket may be in a better position to take a taxable distribution than someone who knows a distribution might elevate them into a higher tax bracket. Beneficiaries of an inherited IRA are required to take RMDs each year, but again, the account doesn't have to be completely liquidated for ten years, so we can help them do so strategically.

There are other situations where a one-time larger sum withdrawal can be helpful, even with its resulting higher tax bill. Someone with a high load of student debt or high-interest credit card debt, for example, might pull out more money from the inheritance just to get out from under that debt.

Ways to purchase asset based long-term care

We see an increasing number of people these days—people in their fifties for instance—expressing concerns about long-term care (LTC). Perhaps that's because they're learning more about what it can cost. Or maybe it's because they've learned of the toll taken—both financially and emotionally—on anyone who attempts to be the caretaker of a parent or anyone else in need of significant nursing care.

The emotional toll is sometimes difficult to quantify, even though very real. As mentioned earlier, I personally witnessed both the mental, physical, and financial strain placed on a family member attempting home nursing care for a loved one unable to afford private care. It's a cliché, but accurate to say that I wouldn't want anyone to have to deal with that kind of hardship.

It's relatively easier to put a dollar estimate on the cost of such care.

Genworth, a company long regarded as a leading authority in the field of long-term care insurance and the cost of services, has since 2004 conducted its nationwide "Cost of Care Survey." Different types of nursing-care services are studied, including at-home services, community care programs, assisted living, and private in-patient nursing home care. The results are broken down by states, then areas within each state. Let's look at what the 2023 survey determined as the median cost for various services in the state of Michigan and several central Michigan communities.

Median Monthly Living Costs[46]

	Michigan	Midland	Saginaw	Lansing
In-home services[47]				
Homemaker services	$5,911	n/a	n/a	$6,673
Home health aide	$6,292	n/a	$5,529	n/a
Community/assisted living				
Adult day care	$4,333	$1,354	$4,333	n/a
Assisted living	$5,050	$4,150	$5,000	$5,500
Nursing home care				
Semi-private room	$10,570	$10,798	$6,844	$10,859
Private room	$11,467	$11,102	$6,844	$11,558

As you can see, these monthly estimates run up rapidly when extrapolated over the course of a year. Now, consider that the average duration of care for women is 3.6 years and 2.5 years for men, and about 22 percent of all adults will need care for more than five years.[48] Even the annual cost of a community-based adult day care program in nearby Midland can cost up to $16,250—considerably less than the cost of a

---

[46] Genworth. 2024. "Cost of Care Survey" https://www.genworth.com/aging-and-you/finances/cost-of-care.html
[47] In-home care estimates based on total of forty-four in-home services hours used weekly.
[48] Stephanie Stearns. Northwestern Mutual. August 28, 2024. "How Long Does the Average Person Need Long-Term Care?" https://www.northwesternmutual.com/life-and-money/how-long-does-the-average-person-need-long-term-care/

semi-private room in a Michigan nursing home, but still a significant cost.

Now, how are you—as a person concerned with not putting that kind of burden on your spouse or your children—going to pay for these possible nursing-care costs?

Here is where our Family Circle planning comes into play. Here is where we try to help people plan for these potential expenses without necessarily buying traditional LTC insurance that might force them to decide whether they can afford to keep that coverage at a time when they're close to using it.

As you can see, I'm not a big fan of traditional LTC insurance.

Yes, it can provide help with costly nursing care expenses, but at what cost? I've seen too many cases where frequent rate increases—sometimes doubling the premium an insured person first paid at a younger age—make it harder to retain this coverage as the time grows closer to actually needing it. Retired people on a fixed income often find that paying the rising premiums on these policies becomes a financial burden.

Worse yet, many LTC policies were sold on a "use-it-or-lose-it" basis, much like term life insurance. Many people who felt compelled to stop paying the premiums and give up the coverage before using it had nothing to show for all their years of paying into the policy. (To be fair, let's note that some combination life insurance/LTC policies today offer a residual death benefit paid to designated beneficiaries. But I'm still not a fan.)

I'm a much bigger believer in financing LTC through a life insurance or annuity structure with an LTC benefit or "rider."

As discussed previously, some whole life insurance policies and annuity contracts today have provisions that allow use of part of the death benefit, or increased annuity payments, when needed for LTC. Some life insurance, in fact, allows use of up to half the death benefit for

LTC, the need for which is triggered by a documented inability to perform two of the six activities of daily living (ADL).[49]

Let's look at an example of how the premium paid on a whole life policy can be leveraged into a considerably larger pool with benefits not only for the policy's beneficiaries, but also possible living benefits (if needed) for the insured.

Let's assume, in this example, you purchase a $500,000 whole life insurance policy with ten premium payments of $20,000 each. That kind of policy might offer as much as $250,000 for health-related needs or expenses. (Your actual premiums, death benefit, and LTC benefits will vary by the product and the carrier, as well as your age, health, and more, but you get the idea).

True, any money used for LTC (or taken as tax-free income via loans taken against the policy) deducts from the death benefit, but this gives you options that check several boxes. You can use the insurance for its traditional purpose—providing financial protection for a young family or a tax-free death benefit to heirs. Or, it could be used as a means of funding LTC or even providing additional tax-free retirement income. Again, life insurance is a multi-purpose tool in which a person could potentially receive value from their policy whether it's used for LTC or not.

Unfortunately, not everyone can be medically underwritten for life insurance. But anyone can open an income annuity contract, many of which today offer the ability to double the scheduled payout when needed for LTC.

Example: A person receiving, say, a 5 percent annual payout from an income annuity might see that payout doubled to 10 percent for a number of years (as defined in the contract) when LTC need is demonstrated. Again, here is an insurance-based option that checks

---

[49] The activities of daily living (ADL) are defined as the skills needed to manage one's basic physical needs. They include personal hygiene, grooming, dressing, toileting, eating, and transferring/ambulating. Source: Peter Edemekong. Deb Bomgaars. Sukesh Sukumaran. Caroline Schoo. National Center for Biotechnical Information. 2024. "Activities of Daily Living" https://www.ncbi.nlm.nih.gov/books/NBK470404/

several boxes, including reliable income and funding for possible future nursing care.

One goal in helping people with the Family Circle portion of our FOCUS Wealth Plan is to bring this plan "full circle." By that we're talking about looking after your loved ones after you can no longer do so, or if your health needs or living needs change. We want a plan that accounts for all of this should the need arise. We want a plan that helps to reduce the burden on a caregiver—most typically a family member—when they don't have to worry over whether they can afford the care a loved one might need.

CHAPTER **8**

Implementation: Put your Plan into Motion

We've now done the planning necessary to set up your FOCUS Wealth Plan. But we're not finished. Not by a long shot.

We've done the FOCUS, gotten to know you and your needs and wants. We've had a chance to Analyze your current situation, to examine the parts of your financial life that are strong as well as those that need improving. We've looked ahead to the pitfalls you might encounter on your road through retirement, and we've talked about ways to move past them. We've detailed how much you could expect to receive in steady, reliable income from Social Security and other recurring sources. We've looked at your projected spending in retirement, then used assets from your retirement savings to help fill the gap between regular income and both anticipated and unexpected expenses. We've addressed the funding of your health care needs and the potential for possible future long-term care. We've talked about strategies that can help you keep more of your money in your pocket instead of Uncle Sam's. We've talked of ways to support the people who mean the most to you when you are no longer here to do that for yourself.

Now we're at the point where we begin to put all this planning into motion. Now is when we make the transition from planning for retirement to actually being in retirement.

Here is where we begin the process of actually turning on a monthly income check that will replace the one you will no longer receive from an employer. Here is where you ultimately decide when you want to begin taking Social Security benefits. Here is where we will help you to do so, right down to the all-important details of making sure your monthly benefit check arrives in your bank account correctly.

Here is where we help you decide how and when you will receive your income. Social Security payments come monthly, but how would you like to receive any supplemental income? In monthly payments? Quarterly? We will work with you to ensure that this income hits the bank accounts you want, and at a time you want to receive it.

Here is where we begin the process of giving you more control over your retirement savings, and more options on what to do with it. Here is where we will work with you to implement the agreed-upon strategies such as, with our assistance, initiating a rollover of the assets in your company-managed 401(k) or 403(b) into your personally controlled individual retirement account (IRA) where the investment options and withdrawal rates are not limited to those offered by the management firm that oversees your company plan.

Here is where we will help you decide from which accounts—and how much will be taken from each—you will withdraw the money necessary to supplement what you need but don't receive from "fixed" income. Here is where we will look at whether to take income from qualified (tax-deferred) accounts, use money from tax-free ones, or likely employ some combination of withdrawals from both.

Here is where we help you enroll in Medicare and make your decisions on when to start Part B coverage, a decision that likely will be based on whether you are continuing to receive coverage from an employer plan or other source. Here is where we will help you consider your many (often confusing) options for Medigap supplemental coverage, or explore the Medicare Advantage alternative. Here is where we help you choose and ultimately enroll in a Part D prescription drug plan that best addresses your unique needs. (This help in making your health care choices, we might add, is something not all retirement firms routinely offer.)

Here is where we will encourage you to actively consider implementing various elements of our tax planning strategy, including meeting with your tax advisor. This might involve moving tax-deferred money into tax-free Roth accounts, depending on when an opportune time comes to pay the tax that comes with such a conversion. Here is where we might begin working closely with a tax accounting professional who can take a closer look at your current and possible future tax brackets to determine when and how much of your current tax-deferred money might be converted in any given year.

We might also begin exploring life insurance options that can produce tax-free income for either yourself (and a spouse) or a beneficiary. Maybe this is something we might pursue immediately; maybe it's something to explore six months down the road. Either way, we encourage you to consider these options for two important reasons. First, it's a way of leveraging a smaller pool of money into a larger source of tax-free income for yourself, a surviving loved one, or a charitable gift after your passing. Second, don't forget that funding for future long-term care also is available through some life insurance and annuity products.

A plan focused on your unique situation

I guess the point I'm trying to make in this discussion is that planning—while essential to a successful retirement—isn't enough on its own. You also need someone who makes sure that your plan is implemented properly. Without taking this final step, all you have is—well, a nicely developed plan.

Consider the development of any major construction project, be it a single-family home or a multiple-story office building. An architect draws up a complex plan, then turns it over to an engineer (or performs regular on-site inspections themselves) to make sure the construction follows the specs.

When it comes to your retirement plan, we believe in being both the architect and the engineer. In both drawing up your plan and then putting the wheels in motion, our goal is to make sure that all components of the plan —all pieces of the puzzle—fit together. We'll not only show you the puzzle box cover—the picture of what the finished puzzle should look like—but actually be there with you to put the thing together.

We often hear from people who come into our office and say, "I'd really love to retire soon, but I'm unsure of how to go about getting health insurance when I leave my employer. And how much will it cost me?" We hear this day in and day out.

We've personally seen the problems people can encounter when the implementation of their plan is not done in a timely manner. We've seen people on Medicare, for instance, encounter problems when traveling without having proper supplemental coverage in place. We've also seen people who delayed enrolling in Part B coverage—people who were still working and covered by an employer's health insurance plan, for instance—incur late-enrollment penalties when they didn't sign up within the proper time frame after leaving the company program.

We've also seen instances in which people doing tax-conversion strategies—doing something they've been advised to do—fail to consider how the money they are converting adds to their modified adjusted gross income (MAGI). Some are consequently horrified to learn that their new MAGI put them over the threshold that brings about increased monthly Part B premiums.

Dealing with retirement-age programs is a new and often confusing thing for people who are experiencing these systems for the first time. Doing research in advance on the workings of Social Security, Medicare, and Roth conversions can be tremendously helpful, needless to say. But there also are times when you simply need a guide, a professional who has been down this road many times and knows all the turns and twists.

At McIntosh and Associates, we want to be that guide. We will work to not only explain all aspects of the retirement puzzle, but work with you to piece together the different components of income planning and tax strategies and health care planning and the diversification needed for risk management. We want our clients to know that they can come to one office—our office—and find that all the pieces of their retirement plan will be put together and implemented properly. And, that this plan will be monitored, and changes made when necessary.

Which brings us to our next chapter.

CHAPTER 9

Updates: When Occasional Change is Necessary

Even after we've put your FOCUS Wealth Plan into motion, our work is still not finished.

Adjustments to your plan may be necessary as conditions change, which they often do. Your living situation may change. Your health may change. Your family dynamic may change. The economy may change, and the market is ever-changing.

Change, it's been said, is the only constant in life. And when things change, we'll be there with you to make any necessary adjustments.

Too many times, we hear clients say, "I have an advisor who set me up with a retirement plan, but now I don't hear from them anymore." We never want that to be said about us at McIntosh and Associates.

Adjusting to the changes during your life in retirement is, of course, a two-way street. Some of the changes we will deal with will be brought to our attention by you. Others might be situations you will hear about from us. Either way, the communication channels we will maintain are as important to us after our plan has been implemented as they were when we were developing the plan.

Our ever-changing way of life

Maybe you're planning a major transition in life, downsizing to a smaller house perhaps, or moving into a retirement community. Maybe you've had your fill of Michigan winters and are considering ownership of a "snowbird" home in a warmer part of the country. Such moves will likely require a significant drawdown from your retirement savings, and we'll be there to help you do that while helping to ensure that your income streams remain consistent.

Maybe you want to spend more of your retirement savings on family, take the grandkids on a trip to Disney World perhaps. Maybe you're ready to invest in a family summer cabin on a lake, or add or upgrade a boat that inevitably goes with such a property. Maybe you just want to spend more money on yourself, free up some hard-earned cash for that dream vacation to a foreign country, or just do more traveling in our great and scenic country. Let's talk and make it happen.

Maybe you've encountered health problems and see some major medical expenses coming your way. Here is where we might review your health insurance and see if your Medicare supplemental coverage needs tweaking. Or, perhaps long-term nursing care looms on the horizon for either you or a spouse. Funding such care is definitely something we'll want to discuss.

Or maybe you're concerned about market trends and their effect on your retirement income or investments. Such concerns were common during the market downturn in the first half of 2022 when the S&P 500 slipped into a bear market (a loss of 20 percent or more from a previous high), joining the NASDAQ that was already entrenched there. We're always ready to talk about these concerns and make adjustments should you feel anxious about the level of market-risk exposure your investment portfolio is facing.

Another part of our monitoring process might involve an end-of-year tax analysis. This is where, often with the help of a tax professional, we look at your current tax bracket, project whether it might change in the next year, and then decide whether this is a strategic time to consider tax conversions (such as the Roth IRA conversion) that might be done without advancing you into a higher tax bracket.

Other parts of our monitoring process involve basic bookkeeping and updating. We also do an annual beneficiary review, which is an important part of our legacy planning. Changes in your family structure due to death, divorce, or (unfortunately) disputes can create changes in the beneficiary designations on your bank accounts, brokerage accounts, IRAs, insurance policies, and annuities. It's important to review these designations on a regular basis.

We also work with people who have trusts and their attorneys to help ensure any new or existing assets are correctly titled within the trust, and that the distribution instructions reflect their current intentions. If you remember from our earlier discussion on legacy planning, any asset that is not properly included within a trust is like a valuable piece of jewelry sitting outside of a vault or lockbox.

Another thing we encounter often here in central Michigan involves the sale of farmland, especially as older citizens look to cut back or move away from an especially grinding lifestyle. Or, as mentioned previously, people will look to downsize or seek a winter home in a warmer climate. People disposing of property often need help in dealing with capital gains taxes, and we are happy to guide them through the process of determining what tax obligations they might face. Or, people who inherit property from loved ones might need guidance on what to do with this newfound asset. We also stand ready to help with these new issues of ownership.

Sadly, the inevitable life-altering change we deal with most follows the passing of a loved one. Here is where we go to work immediately to help a surviving spouse or inheritors resolve estate or inheritance issues as quickly as possible. Here is where, among other things, it's important to understand the possible tax implications of money you might inherit. Clearly, it's better to know the taxable consequences of inherited money ahead of time and before an unexpected tax bill shows up in your mailbox.

Let's keep in touch

We have various ways of keeping in frequent touch with our client friends.

The core way is through our annual reviews (or more should you desire) where we sit down to discuss what is going on in your life, then explore whether we need to make adjustments to your income and/or investment plan. Maybe you need more income, and we will look at where that might come from. Maybe you've found that you're doing better than you expected with your income streams, and you decide you have money to invest and grow for future uses. Always glad to talk about that as well.

But formal in-office reviews aren't our favorite way of keeping in touch with our client friends. We do two social events each year, and even more informational sessions that we encourage people to attend. And, of course, our friends are always welcome to call anytime they have a concern.

We also try to stay connected through informational newsletters, blogs, and radio programs. Each client receives a weekly "McIntosh Minute," an update on what we see happening in the markets or other financial news that might affect our clients. Nolan and I also conduct our weekly *Wealth Michigan* radio program, an hour-long discussion of various retirement planning topics that can be heard on Central Michigan's WSGW 790 AM and Newsradio WSGW 100.5 FM on Sunday afternoons.

But sometimes we don't wait to hear from you. Indeed, you might hear from us if we see market trends that could adversely affect your retirement income or investment plan and believe adjustments may be needed.

Being proactive costs us a lot of time and extra hours, but we are happy to make changes for our clients when we can offer them the potential for greater inflation protection or growth opportunities.

Working to help provide our clients confidence and clarity to have an ideal retirement is what we're here for, and we took the time to make sure we got it done. It's an active style of portfolio management that we prefer over a passive "just flow where the market goes" philosophy. Clients come to appreciate that we are actively monitoring their portfolios.

CHAPTER 10

Picking Your Team, and Why It Should Be Us

And now we've come to the end of this book. It's my hope that in the previous chapters, Nolan and I have given you some valuable insights into the kind of planning we believe is essential to a confident retirement. We also hope we've given you some ideas for adjustments you might consider to any current plan you might already have.

For those readers who've yet to develop such a plan, may I suggest that it's time to seek the help of a retirement professional? And for those who have worries or concerns about the plan they have, may I suggest it might be time to consider changing firms, possibly to one whose emphasis is less on growing wealth and more on preserving and developing lifelong income streams from the assets you've spent a lifetime of hard work to accumulate.

May I also respectfully suggest that you will find that kind of distribution emphasis at McIntosh and Associates?

Choosing a financial team that can help take you into, and all the way through, your years of retirement—however long a period that might be—is obviously an important decision. Trust will be the most important factor in making this decision. So will being comfortable with this person. The team of your choice should be someone who can relate to your unique situation and needs, someone who views you as an individual as opposed to part of a herd.

I believe I'm just such a person, one who can personally relate to the experiences and needs of the people of central Michigan. I say this because I've literally walked the same road as many of the people we see in our Freeland, Michigan office. I've been there and done that when it comes to fighting one's way out of hard times and developing a more positive future.

To bring this book full circle, allow me to revert briefly to the opening chapter as a way of reminding you that where we start is not nearly as important as where we finish.

What I wish I knew then

I was a junior in high school when my life was suddenly turned upside down.

I was only somewhat aware that there was a problem with my family's financial situation. How could you not be with all the phone calls from bill collectors and the meetings with lawyers, bankers, and creditors? But the extent of the problem, and just how and why we were in such turmoil, eluded me.

How could we be so far in debt? My dad was a hard-working, callused hands man who put in anywhere from fourteen to eighteen hours of work a day for as long as I could remember. Yet one day, there it was—a foreclosure notice in the local newspaper with our name on it.

Our land was sold to the highest bidder and all of our farm equipment sold at auction. I can still remember the look on my father's face when his treasured second-generation owned tractor was driven out of our driveway by a complete stranger.

My dad was devastated and blamed himself for the loss. It wasn't all his fault, of course. Crop prices were low. Fertilizer, seed, and fuel prices were high. But he also had made some misguided stock market and investment choices as well, which all contributed to a huge deficit.

I watched, and I remember feeling helpless as my family struggled to hang on to our dignity and the house I grew up in. I had always taken for granted that I would graduate high school and go off to college, but now, I no longer had that certainty. How could we afford it? But the toughest thing by far was watching the toll that all of this took on my dad.

In the end we toughed it out, stuck together, and picked up the pieces. We were no longer farmers as we had no land and no equipment, but we were able to pay off most of our creditors when Dad found a different job.

It was during all of this turmoil that I realized how our problems were due, in large part, to a lack of financial education. My eyes and mind were now wide open, and I became obsessed with educating myself and my family on ways to plan for our financial future more efficiently and effectively.

Long story short, I did go to college (Michigan State University) where I studied hard and earned a bachelor's degree. From there, I continued to educate myself on finances through continuing education courses. In time, I formed my own financial services and retirement planning company.

Today, I've realized my goal of helping other people learn many of the financial basics my own family needed to know during my teens.

Today, our team can show you how much of your hard-earned investment money should be at risk or "in the market." Today, we can teach you the how, what, where, and why of keeping a percentage of your money in a protected asset account, one protected against loss due to market performance. Today, we can show you how to employ a range of tax-smart techniques designed to help you keep more of what you've earned in your own pocket. Today, we can help you choose the Medicare plan suited to you; decide when to begin taking Social Security; consider a hybrid way of funding possible long-term care costs; explain the implications of RMDs and the tax costs of inherited IRAs as well as a variety of other different retirement-age situations that will be new to you as you enter this new, exciting phase of life.

Today, my team and I have the drive, the want, the means, and the knowledge to provide you with the help I wish I could have given my father. All you need to do is give us the opportunity. At McIntosh and Associates, we focus on you—your story, your family, your values, and your dreams.

Let's talk about you

But enough of my story. Now I'm anxious to hear yours.

I want to begin working with you on the development of your own FOCUS Wealth Plan. I look forward to the FOCUS phase, to learn what you've accomplished, where you want to go, what are your dreams. I'm anxious to see what we find in our Analysis of your situation: What are the pitfalls ahead? What remains to be done? We'll work together to find possible Strategies to filling income needs, limiting tax drawdowns, providing healthcare and long-term care coverage, managing the risk of retirement investments and addressing some necessary estate issues. I also look forward to our team Implementing your plan, to putting the wheels in motion as you start down the road of retirement. Finally, I look forward to me and my team continually Monitoring your progress in what I hope will be a long and productive relationship.

But first we need to meet.

That first meeting is when we begin establishing the level of trust that will be so important in this professional relationship. You simply must know that you can rely on the person and team with whom you will work on something as important and personal as a retirement plan that must support you for the rest of your life.

The financial firm you choose should have a history, backed by references, of meeting the needs of clients for an extended period of time. I continue to take pride in all that we're able to do for the people who visit our office. We've been doing these things for twenty-plus years now and we're working on doing more, or doing things even better.

And there are so many different things we do at my company.

We're not just an investment advising service, though we offer that. We're not just a tax-strategy service, though we offer tax strategies. We're not just a health insurance broker, though we do help people find the coverage that is right for them in their Medicare years. We're not just an income planner, though that certainly is a huge part of our process. We don't just sell life insurance and annuities, though my background there can be very helpful when it comes time to consider insurance options for the tax strategy and legacy reasons cited elsewhere in this book.

People often ask how we are compensated for all that we do, and it's a fair and important question.

We do not charge a flat fee to develop an income plan, or to help establish your Social Security and Medicare enrollments. We do not charge extra for discussing tax strategies or legacy guidance. These are all things we consider essential components of your FOCUS Wealth Plan.

We do, however, receive commissions for any sale of life insurance, annuities, or health care coverage that might be components of your overall plan. We also have a fee—1 percent of assets under management—for clients participating in our investment management services.

People also learn quickly that we truly care about their lives and those of their families. We are a family-run company that has been helping other families for almost two decades, and we're not looking to go away anytime soon. We plan to be here for you and your family for a long time, but we also have a succession plan in place for the time (years from now) when Nolan and I enter the retirement lifestyle we've been talking about for years.

I also like the "one-stop shop" concept we've worked hard to establish. I truly believe it can be helpful for clients to know they can go to one place and find answers to all their retirement questions, as well as options designed to help meet all their retirement needs. Simply put, it cuts down on the time required to do all the things necessary to prepare for retirement. Everyone has things they want or need to do in life, and getting your retirement planning done in one place can open up more time to do those things.

Putting all legalese aside, the best way to describe our responsibility—and our core belief—is in the answer to a light-hearted question we sometimes hear from clients.

"Would you make these same recommendations for your own mom?" they sometimes ask. "Does she have these kinds of investments in her portfolio?"

Everyone's situation is different and investment tools and strategies differ from person to person. Our bottom line, however, is consistent. That is, we will do for others the same things that we do for our immediate family.

Which brings me back again to what I saw in the financial struggles of my own family and memories of the way we worked, with great difficulty, to eventually break through to a better place.

The thought that always accompanies memories of that time is, "If I can help someone else avoid that kind of difficulty, I will do everything I can to do so."

Life delivers its share of hard-learned lessons, and I've spent my time in class. Now I'm resolved to take the lessons learned and use them to not only have a positive impact on the lives of my own children, but on your family as well.

It's been said that the best we can hope for at times is to do the right thing and make whatever positive impact we can in our limited circle of influence. I agree with that, but I also believe in trying to widen that circle if at all possible. It's part of the reason I started my own company.

At McIntosh and Associates, we enjoy the work we do on a daily basis. We better enjoy it, because we spend a lot of time doing it. We believe that the way you choose to make the world a better place better be one you enjoy.

Please allow us to share this experience with you.

McIntosh and Associates
8282 Midland Road
Freeland, MI 48623
Phone: 989-692-2200
Email: team@wealthmichigan.com

Acknowledgments

This book would not have been written if not for the inspiration and direction provided by my parents, Ray and Lorie Krohn. They taught me all I know about a positive work ethic. I'll always remember the no-nonsense, "get it done" mentality my late father always had, as well as my mom's integrity, sincerity, and honesty with folks. She taught me even at a young age to always keep my bucket full and to realize how blessed we truly are, and that has spilled over into both my personal and professional life. Her kindness, pure love, and nurturing played a big role in shaping my life, and I will always be grateful.

A special shout-out to Dan Orfin, who was my first manager when I started out in the health care industry. He had a great way of encouraging forward momentum and maintaining a constant energy that I employ to this day.

To Bill and Vicki Ferguson, who gave me at a very young age an attitude to "just do it." This became the driving force in my effort to prove the worthiness of a knowledgeable young woman in this business, one who could do good work for others.

Tony Drake was my mentor in income planning. He saw more in me than I saw in myself and encouraged me to grow professionally, to read more and expand my practice. He also did some great work in coaching Nolan. He was instrumental in helping us realize our comprehensive vision in helping clients.

Paul Carpenter was my business coach. He helped me to focus on my core value, which is time and how to use it wisely throughout the day. He helped me to become more productive in the time I'm given each day, and to devote that time to the things that are most important such as faith and family and fitness and business. He helped me put my values in order and to stick to my plan.

And I will always be grateful to my husband, Nolan. He's always been the brains of the family, and very faith-based. He keeps things in check in terms of what is most important. He's been so supportive as a business partner, and a great, great father.

And last but certainly not least, there are my kids—Haylee, Ava, and Naomi. They are the lights of my life. Ava is the sweetest, most kind person ever. Naomi is my little bit of dynamite, and Haylee is our thinker, the one who studies everything. Together, we've come up with a family motto: "Don't let anyone ever dull your sparkle." What that means is, it's OK that we're all different as long as we stay positive and fun-loving. Life can sometimes be short, so it's important to always look for the positive moments, to laugh and love as much as you can. They bring a smile to my face every time I think about them.

About the Authors

Mindy McIntosh, a lifelong Michigander, is the founder and president of McIntosh and Associates, a financial services firm in the Mid-Michigan community of Freeland. She is a licensed insurance professional offering insurance and annuity strategies to help support their personalized retirement plans. A graduate of Michigan State University, she began her career in the health insurance industry in 2002 before founding her own company in 2004. Today, McIntosh and Associates takes a holistic approach to retirement planning that employs income planning, health insurance and long-term care strategies, wealth management, and developing tax-efficient strategies.

Nolan McIntosh, a graduate of Lake Superior State University, received a doctorate in physical therapy from Andrews University. After beginning his working career in physical therapy, he shifted his interest to financial services and joined his wife Mindy's company where he is a registered Investment Adviser Representative.

Away from the office, Mindy and Nolan spend most of their time with their three daughters, Haylee, Ava, and Naomi, in activities that vary from soccer, softball, and basketball to school theatre productions. Mindy and Nolan both enjoy outdoor activities. They also host a weekly radio show, *Wealth Michigan*, on Sunday afternoons on Newsradio WSGW 790 AM and 100.5 FM.

www.ingramcontent.com/pod-product-compliance
Lightning Source LLC
Chambersburg PA
CBHW050304230526
45471CB00005B/2019